# Consumerism

# Consumerism

## A New Force in Society

Edited by
**Mary Gardiner Jones**
Western Union Telegraph Company

**David M. Gardner**
University of Illinois

**Lexington Books**
D. C. Heath and Company
Lexington, Massachusetts
Toronto

Library of Congress Cataloging in Publication Data

Main entry under title:

Consumerism, a new force in society.

Proceedings of a conference cosponsored by the College of Commerce
and Business Administration of the University of Illinois at Urbana Champaign and the James S. Kemper Foundation of Chicago.
Includes index.
1. Consumer protection—United States—Congresses. 2. Consumers—
United States—Congresses. I. Jones, Mary Gardiner, 1920-      II. Gardner, David Morgan, 1936-      III. Illinois. University at Urbana-Cham-
pagin. College of Commerce and Business Administration. IV. James S.
Kemper Foundation. V. Title.
HC110.C63C643                    381'.3                    76-10106
ISBN 0-669-00705-6

Published simultaneously in Canada

Printed in the United States of America

International Standard Book Number:  0-669-00705-6

Library of Congress Catalog Card Number:  76-10106

# Contents

Foreword      vii

Preface      ix

Introduction      xi

Chapter 1      Consumerism in Perspective   *Donald A. Schon*      1

Chapter 2      Regulatory Trends at the National Consumer Product Safety Commission   *R. David Pittle*      21

Chapter 3      Consumer Protection on the State Level   *Celia A. Maloney*      31

Chapter 4      Consumer Activism and Business Interests in Cable Television Development   *Steven R. Rivkin*      35

Chapter 5      Warranties: A Study of Marketplace Reactions in the Automobile Industry   *John C. Secrest*      45

Chapter 6      Warranties: A Study of Marketplace Reactions in the Appliance Industry   *Daniel J. Krumm*      49

Chapter 7      A New Standard for Business: Positive Participation in the Legislative Process   *Peter T. Jones*      59

Chapter 8      Some Aspects of Information for Consumers   *William Haddon, Jr.*      69

Chapter 9      Management Attitudes toward Consumerism: 1974   *Stephen A. Greyser*      75

Chapter 10      Where Is Consumerism Going?   *Mark Green*      81

Chapter 11      Consumerism Today: A Movement Still in Its Infancy   *Philip G. Schrag*      89

Chapter 12      How to Serve Consumers and Make a Profit   *James S. Turner*      101

Chapter 13        Is the Concept of Consumer Sovereignty an
                  Adequate Index of Consumer Satisfaction
                  in the Marketplace?  *Herbert S. Landsman*                105

Chapter 14        Regulation Trends at the Federal Trade Commission
                  *Lewis A. Engman*                                         115

Chapter 15        Evaluating Corporate and Government Responses
                  to Consumer Needs  *David F. Linowes*                     119

Chapter 16        An Appeal to Tired Activists:  A Radical Looks at the
                  Consumer Movement  *Richard C. Edwards*                   129

Chapter 17        A More Traditional View of Public Policy and the
                  Marketplace in Meeting Consumer Needs
                  *Richard D. Murphy*                                       141

Chapter 18        Current Corporate Programs Responding to Consumer
                  Problems  *Raymond A. Bauer* and *David Kiser*            153

Chapter 19        Epilogue  *Mary Gardiner Jones* and *David M. Gardner*    167


                  List of Off-campus Participants                          171

                  Index                                                    177

                  About the Contributors                                   181

                  About the Editors                                        187

# Foreword

Modern consumerism is a healthy development that has rapidly matured into a movement of national and ecumenical scope.

Once based on feelings of antagonism, consumerism is gradually taking on a participative air, as evidenced by the proceedings of a consumerism symposium sponsored in October 1974 by the University of Illinois and the James. S. Kemper Foundation. The conference marked the first time that consumer advocates and corporate citizens had met in a dispassionate academic environment to exchange ideas and define the future directions of the consumer movement.

The conference could not have taken place five years ago. At that time, few people in the consumer movement and the business community perceived any shared goals, and interaction between consumer and business leaders had been minimal. We felt a forum for both groups to meet and discuss the issues of consumerism in a rational, compatible atmosphere would encourage their future cooperation and interaction, so essential to the continuing development of the movement.

Following the two days of formal presentations by the many top corporate and consumer leaders on the program, attendees broke into discussion groups. The sessions proved to be most constructive, and several fertile ideas emerged, which merit further analysis:

1. Effective consumer redress systems should be established in all businesses.
2. Greater self-regulation practices need to be established among various industries.
3. Consumer impact statements should be made by consumer advocate groups on new federal regulations.
4. Courts of 'economic justice' should be established.
5. Product or service standards should be established on an industry wide basis.
6. More consumer information and education should be provided by business and educational systems.

It is hoped that as a result of the interaction, many of these ideas and recommendations will be implemented by businesses and consumer groups throughout the country.

I wish to extend my personal gratitude to the participants of the conference for lending their ideas and expertise to the occasion.

I hope the ideas presented in this book will prove to be as thought provoking for readers as they were for conference participants.

JAMES S. KEMPER JR.
*President*
*Kemper Foundation*

# Preface

On October 11, 12, and 13, the College of Commerce and Business Administration of the University of Illinois at Urbana-Champaign, in conjunction with the James S. Kemper Foundation of Chicago, cosponsored a conference on consumer forces on the university campus.

The conference brought together about 80 invited participants and speakers, representing the business community, the nonprofit sector, consumer organizations, government, and academia. A list of these participants is presented at the end of this book. In addition to the invited participants, the conference sessions were attended by faculty and students from the university. Nineteen speakers addressed the conference, and their selections are presented here. A list of these authors also appears at the conclusion of this book.

The stimulus for the conference lay in the conference sponsors' feeling that the time was ripe to bring business and consumer spokespersons together in the dispassionate atmosphere of a college campus to share their views regarding the role and likely future of the consumer movement in this country.

This book contains the essence of the conference proceedings, along with summaries of the discussions that followed each speaker's remarks. Also included is an introduction on the origins and present status of the consumer movement and an epilogue summarizing the major trends the consumer movement is likely to follow and the demands it will make on the economy, as reflected in the speeches and discussions of the conferees.

# Introduction

The consumer movement in its present form emerged essentially during the 1960s, although its origins go back to the turn of the century when people first thought to use their purchasing power as consumers to fight sweatshop and other deleterious labor conditions. Since those early days, the consumer movement has ebbed and flowed, frequently reactive to particular marketplace conditions that come forcefully to public attention through some tragedy or exposé.

The significance of the consumer movement as it is emerging today is its broad-range concerns with the functioning of the entire marketplace and the diversity of the groups that flow in and out of the movement at different times. Donald A. Schon, in chapter 1, speaks authoritatively about the significance of movements (their flexibility and capacity to change quickly in response to the needs of their constituents) as compared with organizations that have a greater survival potential but are vulnerable to the dynamics of change that challenge their purposes and functions. He also discusses some of the elements of and obstacles to public learning, which he believes are essential for organizations to experience if they are to remain responsive to the changing needs of the constituents they purport to serve.

The consumer movement has focused on many different aspects of the marketplace, including environmental issues and issues of adapting to new technologies, as well as the more traditional concern with the movement of goods and services. The authors in this book reflect these diverse aspects of the current consumer movement. Philip Schrag in chapter 11 and Steven Rivkin in chapter 4 focus their remarks on specific marketplace transactions that create problems for consumers, and Mark Green, chapter 10; Richard Murphy, Chapter 17; and Richard Edwards, chapter 16 express greater concern with the basic nature of the economic system as it provides the parameters in which the relations of buyers and sellers intersect.

One of the most critical and controversial aspects of the consumer movement concerns the form and types of changes being demanded with a view to making the marketplace more responsive to the needs and concerns of consumers. Here again the authors and discussants have widely diverse views. Both former FTC Chairman Lewis Engman, chapter 14, and Product Safety Commissioner David Pittle, chapter 2, stress the significant impact of the role of government in maintaining and elevating the quality of the marketplace. While Engman points to the dangers of excess government regulation, he also sees an important role for government in policing competition and in providing information to consumers. Commissioner Pittle asserts his conviction that his agency had created a previously sorely missed safety ethic on the part of producers, forcing them in advance of production to explore the likely hazards as well as the marketability of their products. However, consumer specialist James Turner, chapter 12, sees the efficiency of the economy far more advantaged by looking to business as the dominant change force. To him, government can only mandate minimum performance while business can only achieve excellence with systematic consumer input into its decision making. A precondition for the effectiveness of both institutions, however, in Turner's view, is the development of techniques to bring consumers into the decision-making processes earlier.

The problems that confront business in trying to respond to the demands of their customers are summarized by Herbert Landsman, chapter 13, and Daniel Krumm, chapter 6. Their concern to respond to the consumer movement is borne out by surveys of business attitudes presented by Professor Stephen Greyser in chapter 9.

The need for consumer information in improving the function of the marketplace and a schematic way of providing it are presented by William Haddon in chapter 8.

David Linowes, chapter 15, and Raymond Bauer and David Kiser, chapter 18, address themselves to the difficulties of bringing about changes in business and government institutions. Peter Jones, chapter 7, addresses himself to the effective role business can play in the legislative process if it will assume a more affirmative approach to consumer protection legislation.

The question and answer periods following each session reflect the concerns of many participants who ask: What has been accomplished by the consumer movement? Is the consumer any better off today than when housewives in Denver protested trading stamps? Certainly legislation has been enacted dealing with product safety and the consumer is receiving attention at many levels of government activity. But is that really a significant accomplishment or is it merely a skirmish in which frustrated consumers have only been allowed to have a temper tantrum? Is business still ignoring the consumer and only changing when forced by government? Is the consumer movement a dead issue — a passing fact?

One perspective is to view the relationship between the consumer, business, and government as three points on a triangle that interact with and are dependent on each other.[a] The basic relationships between the three systems are shown in figure 1. For proper functioning, the system must be in equilibrium, that is, government providing the protection and service consumers want commensurate with the tax dollars consumers are willing to provide. A similar relationship exists with government and business. This simplified relationship is well understood and the dynamics are evident. Less well understood are the relationships between consumers and business that are necessary for equilibrium to exist. Business is to provide products and services to consumers in exchange for

---

[a]Based on an earlier conceptualization of Alderson, Alderson, Wroe, *Dynamic Marketing Behavior,* Homewood, Richard D. Irwin, Inc., 1965, p. 325.

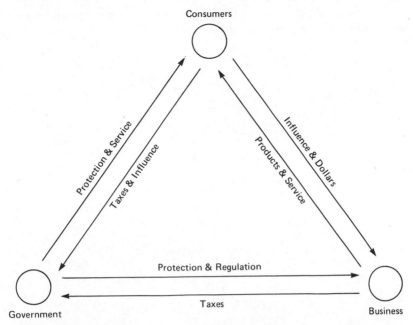

**Figure 1**. Relation between Consumers, Government, and Business.

money. But an important assumption is that consumers have meaningful influence over those products and services.

An interesting hypothesis is that the consumer movement really represents a disequilibrium because shomehow the consumer has lost, or felt he has lost, *meaningful* influence on business as it supplies him with products and services. A result of this disequilibrium is that consumers have turned to government to regain this influence after some limited attempts to restore the equilibrium by directly approaching business. However, the necessity of turning to government, which in turn is expected to influence business, is a cumbersome way in which to restore equilibrium, although it must be recognized that in some instances government influence through regulation and control is the only realistic alternative.

Viewing the consumer movement in perspective we may be able to find an analogy to the farmer who needs to club the donkey to get his attention. It may be necessary to go the "long way around" through government to get the attention of business so it will seriously reevaluate the breakdown in its use of consumer influence over the marketing of products and services. Raymond Bauer indicates in chapter 18 that within business, the donkey's attention has been captured and significant steps are being taken to restore equilibrium between groups. He warns that consumer groups must recognize what he theorizes may be a natural, inherent, lagged effect within organizations, both government and business, between the perception of a need to deal with a problem and the final accomplishment of the needed change.

**Consumerism**

# 1 Consumerism in Perspective
## *Donald A. Schon*

The feature of the consumer movement that most intrigues me is that, being a movement, it is not reducible to organizations: It is not a Consumers' Union; it is not a consumer affairs office; it is not a new agency for product safety; and it is not the consumer division of some company. Indeed, it is not any existing organization. On the contrary, the organizations mentioned are off-shoots the consumer movement has brought into being from time to time. In the words of Tom Burns, these organizations are really epiphenomena of the movement. In that sense the consumer movement is like the Civil Rights Movement or the Youth Movement or the Anti-War Movement. The fact that it is a movement rather than a group of organizations is of crucial importance for the following reasons: social movements are critical to the process of public learning and public learning seems to be the critical policy issue confronting us today. There also are certain difficult and paradoxical problems that emerge from being part of a movement rather than simply a group of organizations.

In 1964 Walter Reuther protested to me about the labor movement, suggesting that a young man coming up through the labor movement today, like a young man coming up through any bureaucracy, has lost the cutting edge, has lost the sense of mission, has lost a sense of what the labor movement is all about. He thought we should renew and revive the labor movement and develop a new sense of social purpose. He envisaged designing a community union movement on the West Coast as one kind of response, to provide a type of training for young workers and their families to renew their sense of mission in the labor movement. Unfortunately he died before he could pursue this idea.

When I worked as consultant to the Catholic Church in Boston, I was amazed to discover the issues raised by the church were essentially the same kind my business clients used to raise with me: What should be our mission? What should be our strategies for achieving that mission? How do we deal with our competition, some of which emanates from psychoanalysis and some from the hippie movement. What do we do about our real estate, which is in the center city? Our parishioners have left and gone to the suburbs; do we follow them or do we stick with the real estate and try to be effective in the center city?

Organized labor and the church seemed to be confronting a sense of inadequacy at the challenges being posed to them. Certain central assumptions and values critical for them no longer held and they did not know what to do. They were uncertain, not only in that they were not sure about the right tactic or how best to play the game, but in that it was not clear what the game was

1

anymore. It certainly was not clear to them that their organizations were not an appropriate response to the game.

This is a time when all established organizations are in that state. One can look at organizations in our society as a kind of map of the problems people thought were worth trying to solve. A paper company was originally designed to produce and distribute paper. A Consumers Union was organized to produce information about product preferences so people could make wiser purchasing decisions. Educational institutions were designed to do what—to be a manpower training institute to satisfy the nation's manpower needs? To produce gentlemen brought up within the liberal arts tradition? To be a research machine on the German model? No. To serve government. To carry out functions for society in other fields, as the agricultural extension service at one time behaved? Maybe. These missions are very different. They arose at different historical periods. Today they co-exist; yet, they are in conflict.

This is what happens when the organizational map begins to be out of kilter with the situation to which it refers. One can think of this phenomenon symbolically as a map of organizations in society analogous to a clear plastic overlay on top of reality. When the problems shift, the overlay blurs. That blur or sense of blur is what we are now confronting: the loss of the stable state, which simply means that the basic assumptions and governing variables our organizations and individuals have built on no longer seem to be quite appropriate to circumstances as we confront them. Let me illustrate the phenomenon with a set of agencies involved in a very special kind of consumer service, namely, those agencies that provide services to the blind.

After World War I, agencies for the blind changed radically. They were shifted from being primarily philanthropic or tied to the church to social service institutions. They viewed their constituents as people who were totally blind and who required certain forms of support. To the people running the agencies, their mission was to rehabilitate the blind so as to optimize human functioning. This was to be accomplished by bringing blind people into the agencies to teach them to read braille and to train them in mobility so they could function effectively as human beings. If you observed the actual behavior of these agencies and tried to construct their practice theory from observing what they were doing rather than from listening to what they said you might infer a very different theory, that "blind people are essentially dependent; they cannot function independently; they require agencies to provide a protective environment for them; they need to become dependent and socialized to these agencies, and, in effect, they ought to spend their lives in association with these agencies, learning to carry out the appropriate role assigned in our society to a person who is blind."

From 1930 to the present, certain things have happened to the population of blind people: Most blind people can now see; most who are legally blind in our society actually have significant residual vision. Most blind people are old; about

two-thirds of them are 55 or older. Because most old people in our society are
women, most blind people are women. Because old people if they are blind also
tend to have other problems, most blind people have multiple handicaps, such as
blindness plus deafness, or blindness plus orthopedic disability. But the population of the blind in agencies for the blind has not been shifting similarly. The
consequence is that agencies for the blind now serve approximately, by my cal-
cluation, 20 percent of the eligible population of blind persons. How do they do
it?

There are certain valves that operate within agencies for the blind, one of
which is called "intake." Any one who approaches a blindness agency who is,
for example, poor, or black, or has multiple handicaps, or is old with residual
vision, finds it very difficult to get service. On the other hand, a delightful,
totally blind child is an extraordinarily valuable commodity and in New York
City the blindness agencies will compete for him. Parents of blind children have
learned to go agency shopping to find the best deal. Because it is essential to
maintain staff and client ratios of the right sort, that is, to keep your people
at least busy, agencies for the blind have increased the amount of the life space
of their clientele taken up with the agency.

We are observing a special kind of homeostasis. The whole system is devised
to keep some things constant—in this case the number of staff and their level of
activity. Agencies for the blind display what I would call dynamic conservatism.
Some people describe resistence to change as a form of inertia, a metaphor
drawn from physics, which is the notion that things tend to stay put, or in mo-
tion, unless a force is exerted upon them. Similarly, agencies for the blind fight
to stay the same. Moreover, what is true for them is broadly true of organizations in our society. They are dynamically conservative systems built around
certain theories of action.

These theories of action tell what the objectives are, what the strategies
are, and what the assumptions are about services and employment. Agencies
fight to stay the same with respect to these theories of action even when their
environment changes. In this effort, they display *selective inattention,* that is,
they systematically fail to observe whatever would conflict with their view about
reality. But when the environmental shift is such that an organization can no
longer defend itself through selective inattention, the shift must be noticed.
If it must be noticed, and if no peripheral change will respond to it, dynamically conservative organizations respond through eruption. The change then is
not gradual, but sudden and disruptive. It is nonrational, usually bitter, and it
involves much human conflict and great waste of resources, often with considerable destruction of the gifts of the past.

In a period of loss of the stable state, the sort of change in the environment
in which agencies function, such as the one just described, does not happen just
once in a period of 30 years; it happens several times. We are living at a unique
time in this respect. The sorts of environmental shifts that challenge our most

basic assumptions are occurring now not only from generation to generation, so we can respond to them in traditional ways—mainly by death, as one generation succeeds another—but they are occurring within a single generation so we have to respond to them within our lifetimes. That is what sets a principal condition for public learning. We simply do not have the luxury of responding to major changes in the environment in the mode of dynamic conservatism and occasional eruptive change, which has characterized our society up to now. What this means is that organizations designed to solve problems, which at some point in the past someone thought were worth solving, need to become very good at learning.

Organizations need to become very good at generating ideas in good currency for the problems that arise. An *idea in good currency* is not just an idea in peoples' minds, it is an idea that is powerful for action. In the mid-fifties we had certain ideas powerful for action that went under names like "basic research," "competition with the Russians," "scientific and technical manpower." By the early sixties those ideas were no longer in good currency. Instead, we had ideas like "poverty," and "social need." Around the winter of 1967, the concept of an environmental crisis came into good currency. In 1964 Lyndon Johnson discovered the problems of the cities, which came into good currency. An idea in good currency is an idea with which it is possible to get resources and to command attention. When you use it in talking to a congressman, he listens. We need to be worried about the environmental crisis, of course; the nation is concerned about poverty, of course; consumer product safety is a major issue for us, of course. Responses to the obviousness of the problem reflect ideas in good currency but ideas in good currency have certain properties. For one, there are not very many of them at any given time. They obey what I would call a law of limited numbers. Second, new ones tend to drive out old ones like womens' fashions. Third, it takes time to get an idea into good currency and it takes time afterwards to get it out of good currency.

In 1959 we had a shortage of scientific and technical manpower. We know we did because the Defense Department's R & D budget was rising. (Jokers at that time used to say that the R & D budget of the Defense Department would intercept the gross national product by 1980.) NASA was just starting. The Killian Commission was formed to study the problem. It did careful research. But between 1959 and 1963 when the commission published its report formally declaring we had a shortage of scientific and technical manpower and recommending legislation to alleviate the shortage, some things had changed. The rate of defense spending for R & D had started to level off. Graduate students in universities had begun to look toward engineering and science schools. We had scientists and engineers walking the streets in Los Angeles and Long Island. But we passed the recommended legislation anyway after the problem had begun to reverse itself. It takes time to float an idea in good currency and it takes time for it to decay. The learning competence of an organization or of a government is in part a function of how good it is at making the rate of generation of ideas in good currency and their decay match the changes and the problems that confront the society.

The effectiveness of an organization (or a person) depends upon its ability to get rid of most of the available information and to pay attention only to a very little with which it can operate, and for which it has a theory. Ideas in good currency are the means by which organizations select what they will pay attention to. They are the means by which organizations determine the problems worth solving. They are not reducible to what is in peoples' heads because peoples' heads contain more than the organization has. In some ways the organization knows more than the people, and in some ways it knows less. With respect to ideas in good currency it knows more. The ability of an organization to generate ideas in good currency is a critical feature of its ability to learn and to be effective.

In order to learn, an organization has to be able to disconfirm some proposition in its practice theory. The blind agency, for example, has to be able to discover that some assumptions it was making about its clients were wrong. If it cannot discover that, it cannot learn. Sometimes events help. In World War II, for the first time, there were soldiers returning from Europe who were blinded. There was nothing else wrong with them. The disposition was to treat them exactly as blind people had always been treated. They came into the general officer's quarters with their canes and banged on the table, and said, "We won't be couped up here! We want to travel, we want to work!" and demanded training to travel and to work. Fortunately, Richard Hoover, a physical education instructor, was there, and he knew something about blindness. Out of his encounter with the returning vets in World War II came the long cane, the first really useful mobility device for blind people.

That innovation resulted from: a crisis, the war, and the returning vets, which produced a new demand on the established and dynamically conservative system. It forced the system to disconfirm one of its prevailing assumptions about its clients, namely, that they cannot show crucial kinds of independence. The agencies that were part of the Veterans Administration establishment did learn that and did change their behavior. The VA blindness system now is strikingly and qualitatively different in its performance from other parts of the blindness system.

In order to learn, organizations also need to experiment; in order to experiment they need to be able to tolerate failure; in order to tolerate failure, they need to be able to attribute failure to something other than the incompetence or venality of the people who do the experiments. I once consulted with a firm, which made potato chips, that was very interested in new products. The president always said, "Good ideas come from the top!" Some of the new products did not work out, however. It turned out whenever a product was a real dog, there was one person in the company who had screwed up and that was the research director. Somehow he was always there when the attribution of blame was required and yet he was never fired. He was absolutely necessary to that organization. They needed that scapegoat because the alternative was the recognition that there were some zones in the experience of the company that were so uncertain no one could know about them.

If an organization must maintain the illusion of its own ability to know, to to know the name of the game, to know the rules of the game and the strategies that work, it cannot tolerate that uncertainty; it cannot tolerate the notion that it cannot know; and therefore it cannot experiment without pushing the blame on some individual. If the blame gets pushed on enough individuals, not all of whom are as masochistic as this research director, people will soon begin to protect themselves, and the organization will lose some of its competence for innovation. Failure is an essential condition in the experiment and a organization must find ways of dealing with it without destroying its innovativeness.

One of the features of organizational learning is the ability to recognize explicitly that a commitment to experiment really does require failure. There are zones of failure and zones of inability to know and there are times when failure is not attributable to incompetence or to venality but simply to the nature of the environment confronting that organization.

Another feature of organizational learning is illustrated by the case of universities and private institutions of higher education. These institutions are in trouble because enrollment demand is not what it was projected to be in the earlier sixties when we started building up public higher education. I was involved in a study of Massachusetts higher education where the rise of university capacity, the investment in new capital facilities, and the investment in new space that took place in the sixties was based on the presumption of an enrollment demand curve by the Board of Higher Education that would reach a projection of an increased enrollment demand of 200,000 students by 1980. Today, Massachusetts cannot reach that projection. As a result, the educational system is overstaffed, overbuilt, and overloaded for its demand. But we also have an institution called academic freedom, which is closely tied to the notion of tenure. Tenure is important because unless professors have tenure they are susceptible to the incursions of a Joe McCarthy. If they have tenure, they cannot be fired. But if they cannot be fired and you are overbuilt for the demand, you are in trouble, particularly if your financial base is eroding, costs are inflating, and students are becoming less predictable in relation to the four-year college course.

Universities are clearly in a dilemma: They hold values of tenure and academic freedom, and also values of fiscal stability and survival. Given present reality, these may be incompatible in that universities cannot get as much as they want of all of them and, indeed, it may be they cannot have them at all. It may be they have to get rid of tenure in order to deal with the fiscal survival situation. But they hold the value of tenure, and, in addition, what do they do with academic freedom if they get rid of it? That is a dilemma, but dilemmas are crucial to learning. Organizational learning requires the ability to surface dilemmas and to resolve them.

The ability to learn as an organization involves the capacity to develop new structures and new systems, and the capacity to generate a kind of interpersonal world, a behavioral world, which is really conducive to valid inquiry.

At the Harvard Business School there are at least two kinds of people: (1) operations researchers and management scientists, and (2) psychologically oriented and organizational development people. In no public encounter in that organization is it possible to talk about the fact that these two groups of people do not talk to each other. Since they do not talk to each other, and since it is taboo to acknowledge this, it is not possible to look at the integration of those two resources to cope with any problem. Since they do not talk about their not talking to each other, each person carries the secret knowledge that he knows something he is not able to say but which he suspects other people know, too, but they also cannot say it, even though it is crucial to what they are doing.

That condition characterizes much of our organizational lives. Ronald Laing wrote a beautiful little book about it, which he called *Knots*. [1] As long as the condition holds, it is really not possible to get effective inquiry between people. For everybody knows that the other knows something that is crucial to what I ought to do but he won't tell me; if he won't tell me that, he probably won't tell me other things, too. Therefore, that person may not be entirely trustworthy, and therefore I ought to withhold some crucial things that I know that might make me vulnerableif I told them. Therefore I will withhold, therefore I become untrustworthy. If reform of the organization requires that people really do talk to one another about crucial questions in ways that entail some additional vulnerability, they cannot do it. So the organization is not able under those circumstances to take the step that would let it learn. The conditions for valid interpersonal inquiry are central for organizational learning.

What is the model by which public learning is designed to occur? The one most prevalent in the sixties was a "rational center-periphery model." The notion was this: An idea in good currency about what the problems are becomes subject to some kind of inquiry, perhaps through task forces, perhaps through individual professors working in universities. This inquiry generates policy proposals. The policy may be subject to experiments, small-scale, pilot efforts. The experiments are designed to test approaches to the policy. On the basis of the experiment, we generate program concepts. Given program concepts, we allocate funding through legislation, and appropriations. Once we have funding, we generate specifications and ask for proposals against those specifications. Proposals may be accepted or rejected through funding. The proposals are designed to get people to change their behaviors throughout the field. The federal government under those circumstances uses the funding very much the way B. F. Skinner uses rewards in training rats, that is , government wants to stamp in positive behavior by rewarding with money and stamp out negative behavior by taking the money away.

That model, which I think was the dominant model of the sixties, had quite a bit wrong with it. It turns out not to be possible to carry out a valid social experiment. You cannot get hold of the variables, you cannot control them, you cannot learn in that way. Every effort at social experimentation that I know, including the most recent income-maintenance experiment in New Jersey, proves that.

If you set up standards and specifications, you have to generate measures of performance for them and if you generate performance measures, people display a very irritating tendency to optimize to the measures rather than to what you are measuring for. So, for example, Congress wished in the early sixties to control the Vocational Rehabilitation program, and generated the measure of "annual rehabilitations." Congress tied funding to the number of rehabilitations per year, defined as "a person in a job for at least three months." How did the voc-rehab agencies behave? They took the best people they could get, the cream of the clientele, and put those people into the lowest-order jobs they could get and never looked again after three months. Then they systematically failed to distinguish between a case and a person, so you never really knew whether you were seeing a thousand persons or one person a thousand times. In all of those ways they were able to push the number of rehabilitations per year up. That problem is endemic to any effort to control behavior through standards. It underlies the problem of regulation, whenever it is possible to meet the letter of performance required without meeting the spirit where meeting the spirit is perceived to be negative to your interest. Distortion to the measure of performance is a kind of distortion crucial in the context of public learning.

If you look for effective learning in our society in recent years, one of the things you notice is the concentration of movements that began in the sixties under the heading of Civil Rights, Youth, and Anti-War. It is very interesting to contrast the learning in those movements and through those movements, with center-periphery model of governmental learning. In those movements there were no clear centers. There might be a center one day in Berkeley and a center in Cornell the next. The centers rose and subsided more or less spontaneously. There was no clear doctrine; you could not find the message they were conveying. There were a family of related messages and they changed. The boundaries of the movement were unclear. Some people were clearly in the Civil Rights movement, some were clearly out. Many more were not clearly in or out. They shifted over time. The movement was a sort of social amoeba that was capable of shifting its boundaries and shifting its spots in response to the issues as they arose and of changing its message in response to the issues as they arose. As a result, the movement was extremely difficult to get at. It was very difficult to attack because you could not discover the center. It was very easy to be engulfed by it. It was not the prisoner of its own organization because it was capable of shifting both its message and its organizational network and boundary. This is one of the features of movements that is of the greatest interest and of the greatest concern.

We should be thinking about organized activity not formal entities. The really important elements for our consideration are movements like the labor movement or the consumer movement and not the organizations to which they occasionally give rise. Movements are vehicles for the development of ideas in good currency; they are learning systems par excellence; they are ways in which theories of action become embedded in particular organizations over time.

It is very difficult to influence a movement because they have no center and they have no fixed message. When you operate on the organizations you are not operating on the movement itself. This is an interesting paradox. The really effective learning vehicle is the movement and not the organization, but the very thing that makes movements relatively invulnerable to attack also makes them enormously difficult to manage, influence, and control. What makes that even more of a difficulty for the consumer movement today is that it is now confronting a series of dilemmas in its own right.

The following are a few of the dilemmas that now confront the consumer movement. If they are a principal stimulus for public learning, these dilemmas ought also to be central issues around which the learning of the consumer movement develops.

Once concept about consumerism is the notion that information is useful. If consumers have more effective information about products and services, they will display more intelligent buying behavior. But if Galbraith is right about the new industrial state, large business firms are becoming progressively more connected to consumer behavior through the media and through advertising in ways that make additional information less and less effective in influencing actual consumer behavior. If the large producing and distributing firms and the consumers are linked together in channels of their own so that essentially consumer behavior is industrially controlled—and we are moving more and more in that direction—the injections of other kinds of information are less likely to be effective.

One of the principal strategies of consumerism is that of advocacy, which is based on the assumption that there are established systems to produce and distribute and merchandise goods. These systems act in their own interests. They often act counter to the interests of those outside the established systems. Most of us are outside. The problem is to organize those who are outside to make their voice effective, reflecting their interest against those established producing and merchandising systems. The role of the *advocate* is that of organizing, providing information, educating, formulating options, and pointing out consequences, to enable those outside the established systems to be more effective in making their voice heard.

What has become very clear in recent years is that outsiders are also crucially dependent upon those systems. The lines of dependence occasionally become dramatically obvious, as in the case of the relations between the energy shortage and the environmental control movement. The energy shortage has enabled the oil firms to become more effective at achieving their goals as they see them and the advocates of environmental control who want to control the behavior of the oil firms less effective, because the present crisis makes our dependence upon the oil firms much more obvious than it was before. In general, in a period of recession and economic squeeze, dependence upon industry and business as a source of employment, under conditions in which it is possible for industry and business to argue that advocacy limits its ability to provide employment, again presents itself as a serious constraint to advocacy.

The third issue is: can advocacy against established business in the consumer's name be effective in achieving more than marginal changes in the existing products and services? Can it be effective in creating new systems and products and services where these are required in the consumer interest? Consider the system for keeping people in clean clothes. What are the parts of that system? It includes, at minimum, the appliance companies, and the textile chain all the way from fibers down to garments; it includes the soaps and chemical solvents, and it includes the service sector, people who clean clothes; and it includes consumers. All of them are interrelated, and their many relationships are quite complex.

In the early sixties there used to be great fights among the textile companies, the chemical companies, and the appliance companies over why clothes were dirty. The textile companies would say it is because you are not using the right detergent for our materials. The chemical companies would say it is because the textile companies are not labeling their clothes properly, and they both would say to the appliance firms, it's because you do not have a system that is clear enough so that the consumer can operate it. When I was a young consultant, I went to the Whirlpool Company, and said, "What you fellows ought to be making is a solvent washer. You ought to take solvent and recycle it and put both dry-cleanable and wet cleanable clothes in it the way we used to wash our clothes in gasoline in World War II." They said, to my surprise, they already had it, but that they were not making it. Why? Because there was one thing that women hated more than anything else and that was ironing. If you brought more dry-cleanable clothes into the house, that would increase the ironing load, and women would not accept that.

In the early sixties wash and wear came out of the textile chain. It turned out that wash and wear fabrics could be finished under conditions of heat and moisture and not require ironing, and that unleashed the coin-operated dry cleaner. Whirlpool and Norge fought to be first. Whirlpool had it first but Norge got in first. When Norge got in with the coin-operated dry cleaner, the service sector discovered it could not survive unless it did something. Service operators either had to become a Norge village or they had to industrialize their dry cleaning operations or they had to become highly skilled, high quality, custom cleaners. There was really no other option. So the introduction of the coin ops. fragmented the service sector

In the meantime we were all having our clothes cleaned at room temperature in solvent machines, which created bacteria-static problems and generated for the chemical sector the possibility of a new product in the form of bacteriastats. That whole process took about two years, starting from the introduction of wash and wear.

If you look at the process as a whole, you can say that we transformed the system for keeping people in clean clothes. But who transformed it? Who planned it? Nobody planned it. Who plans for that system? Nobody plans for the system. Who does plan? The textile industry? Not really. There is a textile association but they really don't plan. Burlington plans, J. P. Stevens plans, Whirlpool plans, Dow plans, and the neighborhood cleaner plans, and, no less, women plan. But the system doesn't plan.

The generation of a new system for keeping people in clean clothes represents, if you like, an ecology of organizations. Within that ecology a new product is a lagged response in one part of the system to something that has happened in another part of the system. That is, coin-ops are a response to wash and wear. The combination of wash and wear and the coin ops, the fragmenting of the service sector, and the bacteriastats made a new system that no one planned or developed. No one thought it was a good idea ahead of time; no one evaluated it afterwards.

What about consumer problems? To what extent are they problems with the shortcomings of existing products and services and to what extent do they require systemic responses? If they require systemic responses—around a system for keeping people in clean clothes, around the shelter system, around the feeding system—the model of advocacy in its present mode will not achieve them. You cannot produce change by businessmen simply by putting their feet to the fire with respect to some property of the product they now make.

A further issue has to do with the fact that an adversary process is likely to generate counteractions. When it does, those counteractions sometimes take the form of distorting the measures, just as in the case of the vocational rehabilitation department. Advertisers, for example, become very careful about the words they use and find ways to achieve the same distorting effects and still meet the letter of the law. Regulators, after a while, become closely connected to and sometimes co-opted by the regulated. Is that an accident, preventable by real vigilance, or is that built into the whole strategy of regulation as a mode of achieving consumer change?

Is a movement separable from a person? What happens to movements when the persons around whom they are built remove themselves from the movement? The resurgence of the consumer movement seems clearly a function of one man. What happens when that man is no longer with us? What are the possibilities for renewal when the man has disappeared?

All of these are ways of talking about issues of advocacy: that advocacy is an adversary process, which tends to generate countermeasures, that the vehicles for advocacy tend to become co-opted by those they are designed to control, that advocacy can produce modification of what is but not creation of something new, particularly if that something new is a system. But if not advocacy, what? What strategies are possible for the consumer movement if advocacy in its present mode is not the strategy or if there are shortcomings in that strategy? There are at least three possibilities.

Those outside the established system of producers and distributors and marketers may take on new membership relationships inside those systems. Examples are the Kelso plan, worker-management models, along the Yugoslav line, and board-management infiltration by consumers. These are alternatives that entitle outsiders to move in not only in the model of adversary control but in the model of participation in the problems of design and policy from within.

A second strategy is separatism—community economic development: build a minicommunity with its own self-sufficient economic system in the heart of Cleveland or in Vermont. We have been seeing a resurgence of Utopianism in our society: "That big complex thing over there is hopeless, get away from it, find an enclave, make it work there."

A third alternative is that of transforming existing institutions. Most large organizations in our country in the business and industrial sector are full of people at the level of management who find their life progressively less meaningful, less understandable, less satisfying, less rewarding. The loss of the stable state is no longer a strange concept. People in insurance companies, in industrial firms, in the business sector, sense this and feel it in their relationship to work, and in their relationship to their families, neighborhoods, and communities. There is a very strong and pervasive malaise within our organizations, which is the internal sign of something very similar to what consumerism represents as the external sign. Consumerism represents persistent and systematic dissatisfaction with what companies do as an output. The malaise represents a persistent and systematic dissatisfaction with what companies are as a process. There is a readiness on the part of members of corporations to participate in a redefinition of the conditions of their own work and a redefinition of the functioning of companies. Such redefinitions could have within them radically different and more significant features than the work experience of most people currently in industry and at the same time remain compatible with traditional fiscal restraints and bottom-line requirements. Whether the transformation of business and industrial firms can take place on more than an exceptional idiosyncratic basis is not clear to me, but there is an internal pressure for such transformation.

These are some of the issues that confront consumerism conceived as a social movement. They are issues around which consumerism as a movement will face the public learning challenges of the present and the next decade.

**Note**

1. Ronald Laing, *Knots,* (New York: Pantheon Books, 1970).

# Discussion

*Comment:* Action for Children's Television (ACT) was started by four Boston mothers originally to raise the standards of children's television. As it developed, we saw the problem was really with the commercial system, so we directed our attention to the commercials. Then we became conscious of the importance of the child's perception of those ads and of the differences between the perceptions of reasonable adults and of slightly unreasonable four-year-olds. As we gave more attention to commercials and to perceptions, we saw that this problem really lay in the type of product becing advertised. In some instances, children's perceptions were not so bad where the product being advertised was lettuce or a very inexpensive item; it was another thing when the advertised product was an expensive or a dangerous toy, so ACT began to focus its concerns on the types of products advertised to children. ACT has been critized by some groups for failing to tackle the problem of violence on TV but it believes that is a separate problem and that people concerned with that aspect of TV should form their own group.

*Comment:* Over a period of years, it seems the greater the mixture of political objectives with economic objectives by the parties participating in the regulatory process, the greater the disagreement and the more difficult it is to achieve an end that all sides can agree constitutes fair play. The Judeo-Christian ethic teaches us that fair play is the product of good human relationships. Yet, the urbanizational intensity and size of modern society along with the dehumanizing technology that supports this make the development of these human relationships more and more difficult. We attempt instead to substitute regulation for working out our problems in a spirit of fair play. All too often we make social decisions without being clear about their economic impact. Shouldn't we have a clear identification of the property rights affected by regulation in order to make progress within this kind of institution with respect to the changes we all seem to desire?

*Schon:* Change is going to be easier, clearer, and more effective, if, in fact, the economic content of that change is clearly identified to all people involved so as to abort numerous discussions, hassles, and disagreements.

*Questions:* What about the dilemma of institutionalizing consumer advocacy in government in order to insure its continuance without diminishing its force; Can consumer advocates be successful at changing the system if they insist on remaining on the outside and refusing to become insiders. Has the issue so far been skirted by labor and management? Who can speak for all consumer viewpoints? Do consumers have inconsistent needs and demands? In view of the problems of information overload, what about the utility of its dissemination?

*Schon:* It is not that social research cannot be done or that institutionalization of advocacy will not work or that we must despair of gaining an understanding of complicated social problems. But social science methodology in the model of physical science methodology is the villain of the piece. It is not that we cannot know but that we cannot know in that way. Part of it is that we cannot conduct rigorous experiments. A rigorous experiment is an experiment in which you hold everything constant except the thing you care about. You wiggle the things you care about. You try to see if you can detect the consequences of wiggling them when everything else is held the same. The problem is that in most situations it is very difficult to know what all the important things to wiggle might be. We do not even have names for these variables. In social experiments the things one might wiggle are interconnected in very important ways, so it is very hard to wiggle one without wiggling them all.

Our knowledge about the interconnections is not very good. This loss of the stable state is just as troubling for experimenters as it is for anyone else, maybe more so because experimental situations have a way of changing out from under the conditions of experiment. What killed off the New Jersey income maintenance experiment was that New Jersey, which had been chosen with enormous care from the point of view of a controlled experiment, introduced a welfare program in the midst of the income maintenance experiment that was more attractive than the income maintenance experiment. That was fine for the people who got the welfare and terrible for the experimenters.

Most social experiments I have looked at turned out to be impossible to evaluate afterwards. For example, Head Start was heralded as an experiment. In fact, experiment is a rhetorical, before-the-fact word. It is only after, when you try to figure out what it has shown, that it becomes troublesome. What did Head Start show? Was it a successful experiment? Was it a failure? What did we learn from it? The woods are full of unresolvable controversy over that question. Some say Head Start failed because Head Start children did not perform well in later grades. Others say it succeeded because it exerted a certain pressure on those later grades to improve their performance. Still others who agree that the later academic performances of the children were bad argue that the measures of performance were in error. Some who perceive that the measures of performance were bad argue that the goals were misconstrued and that academic performance was not the goal after all. The real goal was socialization. One retrospectively reads out of the experiment things that it was not designed to do. Furthermore, experiments by definition are small. Programs, on the other hand, are large and their scale effects are not merely quantitatively, but qualitatively different. The business of running a model city program based on 80 or 120 cities is enormously different from running a model city program based on 7 experimental cities. That says to me that a model experiment is really not available in the same way as it seems to be available in the physical sciences.

We cannot conduct social experiments. That is not to say we cannot know anything about what goes on in society. That does not mean we cannot know anything about children and children's television and the effects of children's television on them. It means that we cannot know in the manner of the experimental method. Then how can we know?

*Comment:* What happens when the research money we have comes from one part of the economy that has a direct economic interest in the answer and another part of the economy that is also interested in the answer cannot afford to do a study to counter the first? Sometimes I think that research is only done so there is an opposite voice.

*Schon:* Yes, that is right. But what you have just done in this discussion is what our society has done. Research to you ceases to become an issue of inquiry and becomes an adversary process. I agree with you that research is often an element of an adversary process. But that is not to be confused with knowledge. Once you have a scene in which there are adversaries, those being advocates against the regulators and those regulating, you have a scene of win-lose competition. The game necessarily becomes political. That is the reality of it. When you add to that the real difficulties of knowing, you do not have someone being the bad guy and someone being the good guy. They do not have to do with competence. They have to do with the realities of trying to find out the context in which we really function. Then the problems of knowledge can become political issues in a way that is downright unhelpful. Any issue of ignorance, any issue of not understanding, can get translated into a fight. As I am sure there will be a fight about inflation policy, I am equally sure there already is a fight about counterinflation policy, and there will be good guys and bad guys. But the fact is we do not understand inflation; we have no adequate theory about inflation and the fight will not advance the theory or the inquiry. In raising the questions about advocacy as a strategy I do not want to have the effect of discouraging people from being advocates. But I do want to raise questions about the strategy of advocacy, whether it is the only strategy, and about the price paid for it.

*Comment:* I think you are confusing the standards of scientific proof properly adhered to by academics with the standards of evaluation applicable to public policy judgments. We may not know, as a matter of absolute truth, whether or not the Head Start program has been effective in alleviating the poverty problem. Because of uncertainties surrounding such programs, perhaps the larger public policy objective of redistributing income ought to be approached directly. But we do know about things like cigarettes, and the hundreds of thousands of premature deaths in which cigarette smoking is a factor every year. We do know that the third leading cause of death in the United States is accidents, usually arising in the course of economic production and consumption. In fact, we know that the overwhelming proportion of death, disease, and physical injury is a product of economic activity.

For example, 46 percent of all deaths are from heart disease and strokes, and a large proportion of these can be traced to cigarette smoking and to a high-calorie, high-fat, high-cholesterol, high-sodium, low-fiber national diet. Yet, in reading the heart disease literature one continues to find the so-called cholesterol theory of heart disease characterized as merely a theory. When one dissects this academic commentary, it becomes apparent that the debate does not focus on whether there is not indeed very substantial evidence in support of the theory. Rather, the issue is whether the evidence is sufficient for us to be 95 percent certain that the theory is true.

That sort of skepticism is perfectly appropriate for the academic world. Surely an essential role of the academic is precisely to be skeptical, to keep questioning, doubting, and investigating, as long as there is any significant possibility that a proposition otherwise generally accepted is in fact not true. The problem is that society also relies upon academics for information necessary in the making of public policy judgments. In supplying that information academics tend to incorporate their standards of absolute scientific proof in assessing the relevance and sufficiency of the evidence, when requiring such overwhelming proof is improper, even disastrous, in the realm of public policy making.

Thus, even though the evidence concerning the cholesterol theory of heart disease causation is substantial enough to make it 80 to 90 percent correct, academics would have us wait until further experiments are performed—experiments which by the way are impossible to perform—that would raise the probability to 99 percent. Meanwhile, hundreds of thousands of people are dying in this country because it is only 80 percent probable that their lives could be extended by actions to change smoking and diet habits. So I think that academic and scientific experts, if they are to be helpful to society, must realize the information needs of public policy makers require a cost-benefit assessment based upon whatever uncertain quantity and quality of information is at hand, rather than an eternal search for the absolute scientific truth.

*Schon:* I feel a real dilemma here. I am a recent academic, and before that, I spent 20 years in practice. Yet, I respond to you sort of defensively because being a university professor I have become an academic. The other dilemma is that the thrust of my remarks really could be interpreted as conservative. That is not my intent. My dilemma is how to confront the issues of knowledge being raised, at least in this zone of the inquiry, without subjecting them to real critique and without having the effect of recommending, in effect, tacitly, at any rate, conservatism. Almost every one of the issues you raised about what you said we know, I would argue that we do not know. I would say the questions about heart disease and the effect of cholesterol, sugar, coffee, and stress on heart disease are really indeterminate. That is not to say there is no evidence that these factors are related. But the fact is there is real indeterminacy about the issue in my view. That 55,000 people a year die from automobile accidents, I admit. When you seek the causes of accidents and try to understand, try to do experiments to determine the causes of accidents, from my memory of issues from the Bureau of Standards, it becomes an enormously difficult thing to do. If it is too enormously difficult a thing to do and if consumer advocacy depends upon certainty (because it is very difficult to be an effective advocate with an uncertain trumpet), that is part of the issue. If you have to blow a certain trumpet in the face of real indeterminacy in order to be an effective advocate, that is a real issue. I would prefer to be an advocate for inquiry and not only inquiry by standards of academic knowledge that involve, for example, rigorous methods that are not applicable. There is a fellow who wants to blow a certain trumpet because if the trumpet is not certain you cannot be an effective advocate. Yet, the issues he wants to blow about are issues about which I know there is real indeterminacy. Now how will I respond to that?

*Comment:* You have not responded to the conceptual problem concerning the *degree* of truth necessary for public policy decisions. Instead, you disputed the sufficiency of the evidence I cited by labeling it indeterminate. You are not as familiar with the literature and the evidence on these topics as you could be, but I am in no way suggesting the necessity of presenting evidence for one's cause be dispensed with.

For example, you listed coffee as one of the several indeterminate causes of heart disease. You may have read that in the newspaper, but apparently you did not read about the studies showing that the correlation between coffee drinking and heart disease is a spurious one, since coffee drinking is also highly associated with cigarette smoking, the relationship of which to heart disease can hardly be questioned. Similarly, there have been claims that sugar causes heart disease. But when the evidence is examined, sugar is exonerated from this particular disease to the extent that the problem is excessive calories from any source, including sugar, in conjunction with excessive dietary intakes of cholesterol and saturated fat. You also mentioned stress, and that probably is an important factor. But as is the case with lack of exercise, there is relatively little that we can do about stress other than to tell people to be cool. However, the evidence suggests there is a great deal that could be done to reduce the tobacco and diet factors, and at relatively small cost, if only we as a society determined to make the effort.

It also is not true that these factors are nearly as indeterminate as you suggest. In fact, there is a rather voluminous literature that describes the degrees of heart attack risks associated with various levels of tobacco consumption and of dietary cholesterol and saturated fat consumption. It ought to be possible, on the basis of existing data, to make acceptably rough judgments as to the contributions of tobacco and diet to the overall heart disease burden, to place a price tag on those contributions, and to internalize the costs of heart disease into the prices of cigarettes and of foods high in fat, cholesterol, etc., so as to create a profit incentive for manufacturers to produce safer foods and cigarettes and a pocketbook incentive for consumers to avoid relatively unsafe foods and cigarettes.

You also mentioned automobile accidents, but in the framework of the problems surrounding efforts to identify exactly what causes these accidents. It is significant that you approach the issue in this manner. There are all kinds of causes of automobile accidents—drunk drivers, sleepy drivers, defective vehicles, poor highways, etc. But trying to solve the problem primarily by having someone at the Bureau of Standards investigate why John Doe ran off the road would almost guarantee that the problem would not be solved. Not that such research should not be undertaken, preferably by the automobile industry rather than by government bureaucrats, but once it is learned why John Doe ran off the road, the real problem of implementing behavior modification to prevent such accidents remains untouched. That is not a problem of specific causes, however helpful knowledge of them may be, but of much more general economic and behavioral incentives.

We've been telling people to drive safely for 50 years now, but we have made rather little progress under that banner. We have told people not to drive while drunk, but how else are drunks to get around? Just maybe an entirely different approach is needed, one that makes the auto industry liable in damages for the $50 billion a year costs of auto accidents. The industry would then have a very strong profit incentive to produce optimally safe vehicles, to mount massive advertising campaigns teaching the techniques of safe driving, and to devote a major effort toward insuring that highways and traffic policing rules are optimally safe.

I suppose your response would be that we would first have to conduct massive studies to determine whether, under these radically new economic incentives, the auto industry would in fact produce more of a net reduction in accident costs than current procedures do. But there is no way such an investigation could be validly conducted and still meet the .05 test. There is no way to predict with scientific accuracy the specific responses of the auto industry to an environment it has never faced. Nevertheless, this new approach should be implemented, not on the basis of specific studies, but in reliance upon a more general proposition for which there is very considerably evidentiary support—the proposition that the profit motive has historically been quite effective in holding down the costs of land, labor, and capital. If that is true, then it also ought to be true that the profit motive can reduce costs to which it has never been applied: the costs of the harmful side effects of economic activity—accidents, diseases, pollution, and congestion. That is a proposition upon which we can act now without having to await the outcomes of endless studies. The most important reason why we can act now is that the cost of being wrong would appear to be relatively small. We are simply transferring costs from victims to those who might (or might not) be able to reduce these costs through the profit motive. We are not increasing the level of cost above that which is already being borne.

*Comment:* It is worth keeping in mind that historically, whether in religious movements or whatever, there is good evidence that as these movements proceed, the pressures for their existence diminish. The feedback is then diminished, and they, therefore, commonly tend to achieve less than their original objectives. The institutionalization, the acceptance in the establishment of such groups or movements and of their activities, illustrates this, as we can see many many times in history.

With respect to the criteria and need for data in making public, and perhaps also private, decisions, we have a very lopsided factual basis for public decision making at present. The government in the pharmaceutical area, for example, is almost in the position of having to prove with certainty an impossibility. It has to prove with certainty that something is not harmful. We have a beautiful example of this with a three-month, injectable contraceptive, which, if the charges are correct, produces a cancer in experimental animals. The manufacturer apparently says they knew about it all along and that it is not a serious problem. But where is the prudence that would tend to protect the public;

Should the decision be weighted on the side of the producer when there is uncertainty about the harm or should it be weighted on the side of the consumer? Finally, on the question of the so-called accidents. The problem is not whether people crash per se, or whether they drive safely per se; the problem is rather the total end result, the leading cause of accidents in the country, the major cause of epilepsy, and so forth. The problem is to reduce those end results. I would suggest that throughout the consumer movement the problem is consistently one of reducing end results rather than necessarily logically starting at the beginning of a sequence.

Why must we always assume that when we have a social problem, the solution is to change people? Usually we have historically done much better in changing the environment or something close to it. We should pay a little more attention to just what our problems are and use those problems as the criteria for success. If we succeed to a certain extent in reducing social problems, we have achieved our objective to that extent.

# 2

**Regulatory Trends at the National Consumer Product Safety Commission**

*R. David Pittle*

The Consumer Product Safety Commission (CPSC) is the newest federal regulatory agency in the country and represents some of the most current thinking in Congress about the need of such agencies for independence and adequate power to carry out their assigned responsibilities.

Prior to the Consumer Product Safety Act, which was passed in 1972, President Johnson convened a study commission, The National Commission on Product Safety, and gave them a two-year period in which to find out whether there was a significant problem in product safety or whether there were just a lot of complaining consumerists who said there was a problem. The study commission issued a report in June 1970, which revealed some impressive findings. It claimed, for example, that each year we could expect 20 million injuries associated with products found around the house, 30,000 deaths, and 110,000 permanent disfigurements or disabilities—which would involve an economic loss to the country of $5.5 billion dollars.

This was not a study report that Congress just stuck on the shelf, paid the tab for, and forgot about—they did something. They passed the Consumer Product Safety Act of 1972, which established this agency with five commissioners and all the supporting personnel necessary (presently staffed with 750 persons) to carry out the mandate to reduce the unreasonble risk of injury to the consumer from using consumer products.

Congress did not mean "eliminate" risk and it did not mean to reduce "all" risk of injury. The act says the commission is to reduce all unreasonable risk of injury to the consumer.

I have a small TV antenna: a special—$1.99. The label directs the consumer to use the house wiring system as a giant TV antenna. The problem is if you plug the antenna into the wall first, and then take the two spade clips of the antenna (as anyone can do) and screw them onto the terminal on the back of your television for the VHF antenna, you can get a severe shock. When this product was first found on the market, there was a direct connection between these two prongs through the wires inside this thin lead onto the two rabbit ears. One of those is at a 110 volts above ground. If you grabbed the hot rabbit ear and touched a radiator or water pipe, something electrically connected to the earth, you would get shocked.

The manufacturer tried to reduce the chance of people being shocked by eliminating one of the wires in the cord. Logically, with half the wires gone, you have only half the chance of hooking up the hot wire to the TV antenna.

21

Had they taken the other wire out, there would be nothing but plastic between this terminal and that plug. It would not have done anything to hurt you—or help your TV reception. The potential injury from this antenna is binary, that is, you are not shocked or you are. When you are shocked, it can be serious if you perhaps injure yourself by recoiling and falling back.

Prior to the Consumer Product Safety Commission's existence there was virtually no way to get this product off the market. No one was geared to seize it, to go into court, or to do all the things necessary to protect the public against an unreasonable risk. This commission's efforts culminated in the rapid removal of the product from commerce. It was one of the first important acts of the commission.

Congress, in passing the Consumer Product Safety Act, also took cognizance of the hodge-podge of safety-related acts that have been floating around the federal government for some years: the Flammable Fabrics Act, the Hazardous Substance Act, the Poison Prevention Packaging Act, and, finally, the Refrigerator Door Safety Act. Our legislation directs this commission to use the authorities granted under each of those transferred acts. If we cannot do the job under those acts, we are to use our umbrella, the Consumer Product Safety Act. Our overall strategy is to use whatever authority is necessary to protect consumers.

The Flammable Fabrics Act gives us authority to require children's pajamas and other garments and rugs and other interior furnishings to be flame retardant. If you have a complaint about the price of children's pajamas because the price is too high as a result of this safety feature, we are the ones you should complain to.

The Poison Prevention Packaging Act authorizes the safety tops on products such as aspirin and oral prescription drugs. This has not been completely well received. Some people who are arthritic or who cannot see well, or handicapped people, etc., may not want a hard-to-open top. Actually, we have not yet educated the public well enough to know that if they do not want it they have the option of requesting the druggist to supply a regular, screw-on cap.

Toys, including bicycles, have been regulated under the Hazardous Substances Act. Hopefully by May 1, 1975 a bicycle regulation requiring that all bicycles meet certain safety requirements such as reflectorization and brake performance will be in effect. Another example of regulations under the Hazardous Substances Act is fireworks. Large firecrackers have been banned for several years. We are now trying to ban the small firecracker, the same ones that can put out an eye or mangle a finger. But the proposed regulation is presently in litigation because there have been strong objections to such a ban. We get letters that say, "you are taking away my right to celebrate the Fourth of July, my patriotic freedom, you are doing too much." We also get letters saying that not only firecrackers but everything—sparklers, the whole works—should be banned, that the government is not doing enough. This illustrates some of the dilemmas confronting our agency in terms of achieving public support and trust.

The most important consumer concern addressed by those who wrote our act was their realization, by looking at other regulatory agencies, that too often Congress has said "protect the consumer" but, historically, has not granted sufficient power to the agency to carry out this mandate.

The Consumer Product Safety Act (CPSA) is refreshingly different. We typically do not have to worry about having to be on the good side of every business we regulate. We do not have to depend on the hope that business will voluntarily stop making an unsafe product. We are in a position to force, to require, business to stop because we have effective sanctions. Most importantly, we can cause the marketplace to pay attention.

The sleeper of the year was Section 15 of the CPSA. It requires all manufacturers, distributors, and retailers, when they have information that tells them the product they are selling, distributing or making *could* be a substantial risk of injury to a consumer, to report this to the commission immediately. They cannot bury the complaint. They must not wait for us to see bodies stacked up or to receive a lot of complaints from around the country. Industry is required to notify us immediately. There are heavy sanctions if they do not. This section is a critically important aspect of raising the level of safety to our consumers.

To date there have been roughly 200 of these notifications involving everything from refrigerators to televisions to tractors to lawnmowers. Manufacturers, distributors, and retailers are calling us up, for example, saying, "I am selling a home jack stand that you put a car on and it could collapse." That is good information to have before someone gets under the car. Today consumers are being warned in advance.

The follow-up to the notice is for the commission staff to look at the product to determine if it could be a substantial product hazard. If it is, we offer the company several options: repurchase it, repair it, replace it, do something to get it out of the hands of consumers. If necessary, the company has a choice; the only thing we must make sure of is that its plan is adequate and will do the job.

Nearly 15 million production units have been kept out of the hands of consumers as a result of Section 15 of the act. That is not 15 million unsafe products. That is 15 million production lots containing elements sufficiently unsafe to warrant a recall. It is hard to estimate how many injuries that is going to reduce as it will be quite a while before we can make that appraisal. However, this notice and recall power is a very clear indication of effectiveness.

It has been our policy to try and encourage preliminary, preventative if you like, responsibility for safety in the minds of business people. We have had several hearings since beginning operations in which I have asked the question, "Before you marketed this product, did you test it for safety? Did you take a look at the long-term chronic effects of what could happen if somebody were to breathe in or were to become involved with this chemical, or this spray, or whatever this is?" The most frequent answer has been "no." Safety, it seems, has

not been a dimension that has had enough prominence in the whole process between the concept of the product and the time when it gets into the consumer's
hands. That must change.

Last year I was speaking with a gentleman who claimed to be a high official
in a company that manufactures motorbikes. He explained to me they were
going to tool up to produce a motorbike for six year olds that would be designed with a small engine. In astonishment I asked, "How can you put a six
year old on a motorized vehicle?" The reply was "No problem, they know how
to keep their balance." "But," I said, "they haven't got the brains to know when
to stay out of the street, when to watch out for other people, how to avoid
injury, when to stop, etc. Why in the world would you want to sell a child something like that for?" His reply was, "Do you know what kind of a market there
is for this product?"

Another case involves a cigarette lighter with a flame that could get to be
anywhere from 6 to 8 to 12 inches high unexpectedly. It was imported. I asked
the importer the question, "Did you check to see if this product was safe before
you imported it?" The answer: "No, I checked its marketability but not its
safety."

There needs to be a safety ethic that must start growing. The private sector
must start considering these things. Consumers are beginning to demand it. This
is a free marketplace. The consumer goes out there and has a right to choose
anything that he or she wants to—even to the point of purchasing a product that
does not have enough protection, does not have any shielding, does not have a
logical design. The marketplace, it is said, will take care of these problems because consumers will stop buying the product and the company will go out of
business.

This is a cop-out from responsible product design. To begin with, we keep
making new consumers every day. They should not have to learn the hard way
that a particular product is unsafe; the marketplace will not take care of them.
Most consumers do not have enough understanding to look at all the important
dimensions of a consumer product they have to buy. They cue up on things like
price, color, and fad. They sometimes ask questions about durability, but safety
is not an item they typically consider. Safety is something that consumers
believe is already being taken care of by the federal government. Or they believe
the manufacturer would never make an unsafe product because consumers have
learned to trust the name. I have researched that specific point and found that
consumers do not question the safety of a product because they have never been
taught to nor would they know how to measure it anyway.

Too often I hear manufacturers say, "If 'these people' would just read the
instructions, if 'these people' would only use half a grain of sense when they use
this product, if 'these people' would only use it like it was intended, then they
wouldn't be hurt."

There is a lot of merit to that assertion. But I have deep reservations about it when the manufacturer knows and can predict that some normal consumers will "misuse" the product. Take the case of consumers who will tilt over a lawnmower while it is still moving because it is clogged with wet grass in it. While the blades are still rotating, some consumers will stick their fingers in to free the chute. I cannot tell you exactly how many hundred people get their fingers cut off, but it is too many. It is a phenomenon that is widely known.

There is much need for a safety ethic, a moral responsibility on the part of the person who designs or manufactures the product to take into account what the actual behavior of a consumer is. They should consider what the average person is likely to do rather than to build a product and then say, "Consumer, change your behavior to match my product." That is like handing a child a gun and telling him or her not to pull the trigger. You can predict with a high degree of certainty that the trigger is liable to be pulled. The responsibility should not be shifted to the person who does not understand or does not know.

Product safety has to start at the top of a company. Chief executive officers of companies should assume full responsibility for whatever goes out their door. As a policy, the five of us at the commission have voted unanimously that when we believe a criminal violation has occurred, we will not hesitate to seek criminal sanctions against the chief executive. One large company executive has told his staff he was not going to jail on a Section 15 (b) violation, and that any possible substantial product hazards should be reported to the commission immediately.

We are not in the business of putting people in jail or of seeking fines. That is certainly not my intention. We are in the business of reducing any reasonable risk or injury to the American consumer, something that has not been addressed before in our 200-year history. We will use every arrow in the quiver given to us by Congress in order to bring that about. That is one of our responsibilities.

I am particularly proud of our effort to open up this regulatory agency so the people we are trying to help as well as those we regulate know what is going on. When a CPSC employee has a meeting with someone outside the agency, the details are listed on a calendar at least a week in advance, and the calendar is mailed free of charge to anyone who wants it. Hence, the world knows where, when, and why one of our staff is talking with a representative of industry, a consumer organization, or another government agency. If interested, members of the public usually can go and listen and, when practical, participate. This is terribly important. When I was on the "outside," I was positive that every agency in the government was selling out. Why? Because no one could ever find out what went on in the meetings. I suspect no one ever closed the door— they just never told anyone where it was, and that is effectively closing the door.

Most of the people in the federal government I have met are conscientious, dedicated public servants. But from the outside, when the door is closed or when the meetings go on that outsiders do not know about, it is easy to be positive that

there is "hanky-panky." During the last couple of years the news has carried
enough stories where something did go on, and it is, of course, easy to generalize.

The Consumer Product Safety Commission has adopted policies that are far-
reaching and significant in terms of greater openness of the whole regulatory process to the public. Because of the way regulators operate, decisions are based on
a broad spectrum of information. If you do not use broad information to make
decisions, you are a bad regulator. Given that, I rely on information from our
staff. Therefore, it is whom they listen to that concerns me. There is nothing
wrong with a representative of any trade association or any manufacturer's group
coming in and telling us what their problems are, how they view an issue that we
are about to vote on. After all, they have a very heavy stake in the issue and
they have an important view to be heard. But it is important that anyone else
who wants to listen to what we are listening to has an opportunity to come and
disagree at the time when all of those pieces of information are brought together. This is the time when the staff decisions are being made.

There are some who say we will never make it with the goldfish-bowl policy
we have. But although we may need to change the water a little, so far there
are no cracks in the structure and we are still intact. I encourage any of you in
the room who works at other government agencies, whether it be state, federal
or local, to try it. It is really no problem to let consumers in. They do have a
stake in what you are doing. Let them know what is going on. A problem
they have always suffered with is that they do not have enough information to
make an intelligent complaint. Hence, they wind up stamping their feet. Then
of course you can very logically say, "You are just an emotional consumer, what
do you know?"

It is not always true that when you open the door everyone is going to
come in. But when they want to come or want to know what was discussed
they have the opportunity. Our meeting logs are open to the public. This helps
the person in Montana. After reading in our public calendar that a particular
meeting will take place, you can write to the secretary of the commission and
request a log of the meeting, which discusses in detail what went on.

When I lived in Pittsburgh, I often read of violations of the county pollution standards by some of the steel mills who were later fined a few hundred
dollars. There was not much incentive to reduce the pollution. In fact, the
mills would save more money by polluting every day and paying the small fine.
Why was the fine so small when the limit of the sanctions were much higher?
I tried to go to one of these meetings in which the environmental law enforcers
met with the mill to discuss penalties. I found I could not. I also found the possible penalty was much greater than $300. Consequently, I concluded, "Some-
thing fishy is going on in there."

Now I am on the inside, and I see it from a slightly different view. I have
discovered what happened. Lawyers have a tendency to be straight with one
another—the good ones that is: very frank and open. Here is how I see the usual
process working:

Government lawyer calls up company lawyer and says, "We've got you, and we want a $10,000 fine."

Company lawyer calls back and says, "You haven't really got us; you are a little bit weak on some of the facts. You certainly don't want to go to court. It costs tax dollars; it costs this; it costs that. Why don't I come in and we will talk about it? Oh, by the way, I don't want to talk about this in front of anybody because I don't want any liability. I mean I'll admit to you that we could be in violation, but I don't want to tell anybody else that we are. And if you'll reduce the fine to $1,000, we can be done with the matter."

So they come together and they sit down in a closed room. Company lawyer sits across from government lawyer and says, "What have you got?" Whatever it is, they start arm wrestling over the evidence and the law. Company lawyer finally offers a concession: "We will agree not to do it anymore and we'll say we never did it. Take a thousand dollars and be happy because that's more than the government will get otherwise. I could drag this thing out for three years because my due process rights allow me to appeal and delay and present new information and whatever else I can think of."

What does the public think when they come out from that meeting with a resolution of a $1,000 fine? I was positive that someone got another thousand under the table. Now that I have seen the process from the inside, I know it never happened. Wouldn't the public trust be greatly enhanced if the public were allowed into the meeting.

Our experience is that the first time this happened, the company's lawyer called up and requested a negotiation meeting. We agreed provided that it was an open meeting. The company called back, and said, "I'm not coming. See you in court." A couple of days later they wrote us a letter agreeing to do whatever we thought needed to be done.

I do not know if we can always tough it out like that; going to court means expense and delay when the public's safety is involved. But our policy is that when negotiations are going on, they have to be open to the public. If government is there working on behalf of the consumer, consumers have a right to see what is going on.

I also have concern for the safety and the rights of the manufacturer, the distributor, and the retailer. It would be unfair to punish them in a public meeting and have them prosecuted in the press, etc. We are not there to do that. We are, however, simply saying that they must reduce the unreasonable risk to consumers, and we will not heitate to use any of the enforcement tools given us by Congress if voluntary action is not swift and adequate.

I do not know how well it is going to work as we are only a year and a half old; I believe it will, of course. If you do not know what we are doing you cannot criticize us. A number of outside observers agree it is important that the government operate in a way that everyone can see it operate. If they think we are doing something wrong, we should be blasted. That is as important as it is to get a pat on the back.

# Discussion

Concern was expressed that large firms, in conjunction with the Consumer Product Safety Commission (CPSC), would set standards so high that small firms would be prevented from entering or remaining in the market.

*Comment:* I would hate to see you implement a policy of safety regulation contingent upon *no* competitors ever being eliminated from the marketplace. This does a disservice to consumers who need to be protected from dangerous products.

*Questions:* How much safety should consumer products have, and at what costs? Is the consumer better off with competition and possibly less safety or greater safety and possibly less competition? Who is to determine the answer to these two questions?

*Pittle:* Congress required that we consider the economic impact of every one of our rule-making decisions. Specifically, we must consider the means of achieving the objective of our regulation while minimizing adverse effects on competition consistent with the public health and safety. Let me assure you we do undertake these considerations. In passing, I should point out that these considerations are probably not relevant in the context of substantial product hazards or imminent hazards under the CPSA. In these latter cases, the law directs the commission to get highly dangerous products out of the hands of consumers but is silent with respect to minimizing adverse economic impacts on companies. The reason for this silence seems obvious. A company that, through its own negligence, places consumers in serious personal danger should not be permitted to avoid the consequences of its actions simply because it would cost them a lot of money to do so. While I am troubled if a company says the recall of its product containing a serious hazard will cause the company economic harm, I don't feel that I can legally or morally refuse to insist that the company remove unsafe products already in the hands of consumers. On the other hand, if the CPSC is going to come out with a standard and the standard is going to be difficult to meet, then we can, and I think we must, take a serious look at economic consequences. If the standard is severe and it could put half of the small companies out of business, then we would have to take another look at it to see if that standard hasn't somehow been geared for large companies with relatively little corresponding benefit for consumers.

It would be better if there were a performance standard that could be associated with all potentially hazardous products. Standards are of long-term importance and impact on society because, rather than simply removing products from the marketplace as bans do, standards are used as important guidelines for all manufacturers to produce goods that provide adequate safety for all consumers.

But I disagree with those who say the voluntary standards systems has made standards so high that people can't live up to them. Quite the contrary. Voluntary standards often have been so low that everyone could live with them. That's because it's done via consensus, which at times is a polite way of saying lowest common denominator. I can't say all of them are like that. But the process itself tends to deliver just that: if everyone at the table feels there ought to be a certain size, shape, or temperature to provide adequate safety, generally companies are not going to agree unless their manufacturing process can adapt to meet these requirements very easily.

The voluntary process for writing standards in the past used to involve someone sitting down and asking those who wanted to be involved in writing a standard on widgets to come and sit at the table. You know who was going to be there: companies with an economic interest. Unfortunately, that process did not include many consumers.

Who wants consumers anyway? What do they know about the technical things? Besides, they can never get off from work to attend meetings. Consequently, their views seldom got cranked into the process. The process is different now. We require, according to regulations under the Consumer Product Safety Act, the person who heads the table to give all interests a chance to come and participate and have their comments heard, and, if necessary, the person must pay expenses for those who are otherwise unable to attend. Of course, there is no guarantee that persons who are thus able to attend will necessarily get their way, but all their views will be considered by the commission before we promulgate the standard.

Standards are very important. They have the longest term effect of all our regulatory tools and, as I mentioned earlier, when the commission undertakes standards development, I do consider the economic impact on industry of such development. As to helping small companies, I'm very much concerned about the effect on small companies from these standards. (See Figure 2–1 concerning the interaction between products and consumers.)

In regard to the issues of cost-benefit analysis and the secondary effects of lost work, hospitalization, and other social costs, economists have to compare dollars of cost to benefits that often are not easily measured. What is it worth not to be injured or killed and how do you quantify that benefit?

|              | Good Consumers                          | Bad Consumers                          |
|--------------|-----------------------------------------|----------------------------------------|
| Safe Products | Accidents<br><br>(difficult to reduce) | Primarily consumer behavior problem<br><br>*Education |
| Unsafe Products | Primarily product problem<br><br>*Regulations<br><br>*Product recalls | Product and behavior problem<br><br>*Regulations<br><br>*Product recalls<br><br>*Education |

**Figure 2-1.** Injuries Resulting from Product and Consumer Interactions and Appropriate Remedies (See Asterisks).

# 3

## Consumer Protection on the State Level
### Celia A. Maloney

State consumer protection agencies across the country have assumed a leadership role in protecting our consumers. It became obvious in the late sixties that the attitude of "let's let the federal government do it" was not going to resolve consumer abuses. The federal government seems less than enthusiastic about consumer protection. The Justice Department and the Federal Trade Commission have called a halt to their antitrust activities. Our right to choice in the marketplace has been undermined. A vacuum was created that state legislatures across the country stepped in to fill.

The consumer protection functions of state government have increased. There are many new laws to be enforced and consumer affairs departments are being funded and encouraged to develop consumer education programs and new legislative initiatives. This activity is just beginning. The consumer protection function of state government is becoming more important. A survey of legislation introduced and passed across the country in our state assemblies indicates this is an area where state government is leading the way.

There are many different ways to approach this role. Some states have created a new consumer agency; others have assigned this function to an existing bureaucracy. In Wisconsin the Department of Agriculture issues rules and, along with the Department of Justice, enforces consumer protection laws. The entire system is computerized and coordinated so you have a degree of cooperation between state and local agencies. In New York there is a Consumer Protection Commission that acts in an ombudsman capacity. This commission is required to represent the consumer interest at utility rate hearing cases, for example. In other states, the Attorney General's office has complete jurisdiction over consumer protection.

The problems any state consumer protection agency faces are: (1) Who enforces the laws (the Attorney General's office or the consumer affairs agency or both)? (2) What are the consumer agency's powers vis-à-vis the other departments in state government—do we have the right to intervene in administrative hearings on behalf of the consumer interest and what effect will this intervention have? (3) What is our relationship to the regulatory functions of government?

How much of our limited resources should be devoted to research and developing legislation and how much of our time and staff should be spent on individual cases? If we look at the long-term solutions and ignore the immediate individual problem, what happens to our agency? Do we impair our political usefulness with this attitude?

Another difficulty a consumer protection agency faces is maintaining and increasing its political support. This means going to the committee-at-large and developing that support. The Department of Mental Health, The Department of Transportation, will exist no matter how the general public views them. The Department of Consumer Affairs will not. This department has many powerful enemies and, therefore, we constantly have to beat the drums for support. Public relations is not an ego trip for a consumer affairs director—it is crucial to his or her existence and effectiveness.

The consumer is an individual. He or she goes into the marketplace singly not as a group. The consumer protection agency or agencies of state government are not representing a well-organized constituency. Because our target group is so diverse and disorganized we have to operate on many fronts. We cannot really set up an administrative system that will operate almost by itself. A high degree of institutionalism is not possible in consumer protection. This is our strength— we have to remain flexible and alert to the ever-changing conditions of the marketplace. New laws will be needed tomorrow for the abuses of today. It is our job to identify those abuses, to publicize them to get public support for a remedy, to write a good bill—convince the individual legislator of the political wisdom of supporting it, and, finally, to set up a system for enforcing that law, which insures our citizens fair and consistent protection.

We really are the gadflys of the bureaucracy. We have to be alert to the policies of the bureaucracy and their effect on consumers at the same time we are watching the marketplace and correcting unfair practices. Our target is a constantly moving one. This alone should keep us from settling comfortably into the bureaucracy.

# Discussion

*Questions:* Is preemption by the federal government of consumer protection regulation a good or bad phenomenon? What is the likely effect on state programs if the Consumer Protection Act is passed by the federal government creating a federal consumer advocate? How do state consumer protection programs relate to local and federal programs? What resources are available for these programs? Isn't coordination essential and shouldn't business support such coordination as in their best interests? How does Ms. Maloney establish priorities for her work? What information can she get about the incidence and scope of consumer problems, and can some form of computerization of the data be developed? Isn't consumer protection doomed to failure if it simply accepts the economic system without concerning itself with the underlying viability of the system? Is government playing games with consumers just as business is sometimes accused of doing by creating consumer affairs offices or special advisers to the governor, typically attractive women, who are given fancy titles but no real powers and resources?

*Comment:* There is a real need for coordination of effort and a sharing of expertise and data among federal, state, and local consumer protection programs to avoid duplication of effort and also to avoid inconsistent regulations that are an impossible burden on business. A major component of this coordination should be the creation of a central research and analysis institute—preferably university based. This institute would service private consumer groups, local governmental consumer protection groups, and consumer protection officials with systematic data on the incidence and scope of consumer problems. It would provide various regulatory solutions in effect among the several states, and an analysis of the effectiveness and costs of different regulatory solutions to both government and business.

State consumer protection programs—even with their limited resources—are not necessarily tokenism. In Illinois they provide individual consumers with a place to go with their complaints and to get action where possible. It is true they should have powers to intervene in proceedings where consumer input is essential to effective decision making since appearing *amicus* has relatively little value. Indeed, in many areas of consumer problems, state action can be quicker and more directly responsive to individual consumer problems than can the Federal Trade Commission, which must concentrate its resources on national practices of concern to broad segments of the population.

There is no simple answer to the planning and political problem that confronts state and local consumer protection agencies because of their need to respond to the problems presented to them by their individual constituents and their need to establish some priorities to allocate their very scarce resources most effectively. Immediate accountability is essential to make sure they are being responsive to real ongoing problems but it can also skew their priorities in trying to deal with problems that are widely applicable and cause serious harm to both the long- and short-range interests of consumers. Truly long-range, indirect problems stemming from the type of economic system we have or from the dysfunctioning of our competitive systems are beyond the purview and scope of state consumer protection programs.

# 4

## Consumer Activism and Business Interests in Cable Television Development

### Steven R. Rivkin

When I learned economics from Paul Samuelson's text, it seemed that scarcity of goods and services was the great engine of a free economy, powering everlasting drives to expand production to meet demand, to determine reasonable prices by a process of vigorous bargaining between willing buyers and willing sellers, and to insure quality and innovation through the readiness of competing producers to satisfy unmet consumer demands.

Today, I doubt that anyone finds that rugged model the perfect key to rational and efficient economic behavior. First, the scale and complexity of organization needed to produce and distribute demands market stability. Second, social values dictate that people on food stamps should not be gulled into consuming more and more potato chips. Third, everyone's passion to get more of what he "wants the most" can spiral out of hand, as double-digit inflation saps the people's ability to get what they need, let alone what they want. It is in everyone's interest to find ways to avoid a beggar-your-neighbor approach to production that leaves the consumer both fat and hungry at the same time.

In the New Deal days, the proper solution in many people's minds was government intervention in the economy. To the economist Arthur R. Burns in 1936, the answer lay in the powers of administrative bodies to make

. . . decisions concerning the relative importance of efficiency and other social aspects of production, the most desirable distribution of income, and, more particularly, of the benefits and burdens of unforecastable disturbances of economic conditions.[1]

He found government regulation, under the circumstances, "the best instrument of social control"—a view that many might challenge today.

In coping with the advent of new broadband communications technologies—principally cable television, about which I counsel foundations, consumer groups, cities, and franchise applicants alike—Congress and its instrument the Federal Communications Commission have labored mightily to avoid coming to grips with key regulatory issues. In this effort, federal regulators have been aided, abetted, and prodded by both businesses and consumers to meet the difficult task of reorganizing American communications systems by simply throwing away the key.

In the process, everyone seems to have foresworn allegiance to what the economist Joseph Schumpeter called the single most important form of competition: "the competition from the new commodity, the new technology, the new source of supply, the new type of organization." The faith of an open society "that tomorrow will produce a better than the best" has been abandoned for the grimy pursuit of what we Washington regulatory lawyers like to kid ourselves as being "responsible" regulatory behavior.

In establishing policies for the development of cable television, the regulatory process has, to a far larger degree than warranted, imposed suffocating burdens on both producers and consumers, blocking the novel potential of broadband telecommunications to serve modern society. For more than a generation, it has been possible to send simultaneous signals between two points via electronic means. As soon as a long-distance telephone service became commercially feasible, using coaxial cable to carry multiple messages along a common path, direct delivery of large quantities of information to business and home terminals was a natural next step. As a result of this and accompanying strides in television and computer technology, an endless variety of sophisticated services has come within reach through broadband telecommunications.

No more than 10 percent of the nation's homes are wired for cable. Most are located in scattered small communities, and service is rudimentary at best. A market of scale for programs and hardware alike has yet to develop, and the costs of extending and improving service for an appreciable portion of the nation would amount to billions of dollars, maybe tens of billions. In today's economy, that money is simply not around, and no regulatory solution yet in view has offered the prospect that it soon will be.

**Barriers to Growth**

It is paradoxical, in a society so marked by faith in its technology, that an innovation promising so much should be so long delayed. That paradox is only understandable—although no less perplexing—in light of the bitter economic rivalries countenanced by impotent regulation that dilute and frustrate cable's long-term potential for service. Recognizing this dims the medium's otherwise bright future, presenting a Hobson's choice between a benefit compromised and none at all. Because there is much dissatisfaction with mass television, it has been tempting to rationalize the failures of regulation as inevitable and on balance acceptable. By and large, that has been the reaction of both the cable industry and consumers alike—at least until the recent capital crunch cast a pall on even that flawed promise.

The paradox of cable's shortcomings is rooted in the conflict between its revolutionary capacity and the hardships of gaining entry into the highly de-developed and heavily regulated telecommunications field. If cable had arisen in a competitive void, like that enjoyed by the Bell system at the end of the nineteenth century, there would be little to block its rapid development to serve an eagerly responsive consumer market.

Today's economic facts appear otherwise. The future business of approximately 700 federally licensed commercial broadcast stations, this year generating more than $4 billion in advertising revenues, and the primacy of the nation's telephone systems in point-to-point service are both threatened by competition from an emerging cable medium. Moreover, other weighty forces—hardware manufacturers and producers and distributors of entertainment products—rely on established demand patterns. It should come as no surprise, therefore, that cable television's older siblings should try to throttle the infant in its crib. Given the magnitude of capital needed to foster growth, that has not been too hard a task.

Public regulatory bodies have only recently begun to respond forthrightly to these conflicts over weighty prerogatives and big money. The prevailing distribution of regulatory power shelters established interests and relegates emerging entities to their own ingenuity, usually in isolation from purposeful public controls. Often, the best the FCC can do is to turn a blind eye towards developments in the growth of the industry that fall far short of any rational design for its future.

Before the Federal Communications Commission, broadcast television is ten times bigger economically than cable, and by and large gets ten times more protection. In recent years, as charges of White House manipulation of the media have become more pronounced, cable's potential has become more prominently featured in public policy debates, but close observers cannot help the feeling that most of cable's new prominence comes as a stick to beat the broadcasters rather than a recognition that society has an important stake in its growth and refinement. In the cynical capital, the ground rules for this kind of a game are never forgotten by the players, and, like the croupier says, the game continues.

At the root of the regulatory problem is the fact that the authority for federal regulation—the Communications Act of 1934—was passed long before possibilities of wired distribution of information were appreciated. In the meantime, broadcasters have risen to affluence and influence in every congressional district, and it is not surprising the act has never been amended. Thus, cable initially arose as a creature of municipal and county efforts, often highly permissive, to expand locally available television options. Only when the magnitude and versatility of this cable service was perceived by broadcasters to threaten their protected markets did the FCC wake up to cable's presence. This the commission did in 1966 by stopping its growth, operating under a Supreme Court construction that allowed the extension of regulation under the communications act to those activities of cable that are "reasonably ancillary" to the regulation of broadcasting.

In the ensuing years, the Court has resolved cases coming before it dealing with cable with extreme displays of agony, repeatedly calling on Congress to legislate affirmative standards for cable development. So far, all prospects of legislative revision have died, although few doubt that anything short of a statutory overhaul will ever provide a stable framework for cable's long-range growth.

Thus, the definition of what cable should be—of what services it should provide and how fast it should grow— has been frustrated. To the extent the commission has been able to face these issues, it has adopted philosophies that keep the medium's promise alive but by and large defeat its versatility. The commission intones the doctrines that cable should not be allowed to threaten the integrity of broadcasting, that it should "supplement" and not "supplant" broadcast television, and—most recently and ingeniously—that "it should operate as a local outlet by cablecasting original programs."

Into that last, innocuous bit of doctrine, much legerdemain has been worked. The so-called "mandatory origination" rule—first issued in 1969, upheld by the Supreme Court, and never applied because it managed to outwit its own proponents—became the basis on which the commission has sought to "shoehorn" cable into the nation's communications structure. By imposing public interest requirements on cable systems—obligations to insure public assess, technical quality, and system expansion in addition to original programming—the commission has attempted to find a basis for cable's legitimacy in the common interests of consumers for services and the cable industry for regulatory benefits that can assure its growth.

### Forging an Industry-Consumer Alliance

That perception is surely the key to cable's future, but it is subject to more than one definition. In 1972 the commission established a comprehensive regulatory framework for cable—still tied to its "reasonably ancillary" authority—by which cable growth in big cities was theoretically permitted to resume through limited rations of additional television from other broadcast markets. (So far anticipated growth has been sluggish due to capital shortages and investor disinterest, and now the industry is turning to "pay-cable" to keep itself afloat.)

The industry-consumer alliance propounded by the FCC represents a cover for some sort of perverse anticonsumer subsidy. Broadcasters would get most, cable operators some, and consumers very little of what the FCC has to offer.

Thus far, the FCC's design for cable growth has emphasized that cable systems must be "good citizens" as the condition for gaining enough regulatory protection (access to imported broadcast signals) to survive and to grow rapidly enough to pay out on borrowed capital. The definition of good citizenship involves accepting a role as a mere complement to the existing broadcast system, foreclosing the really attractive prospect that subscriber-supported broadband systems can become the nation's primary means of communications.

The "mandatory origination rule"—now in suspension at the FCC and under review—is the joker. By accepting the responsibility of itself delivering programming to subscribers on its own channel, the cable operator becomes a broadcaster himself. The costs of origination are a burden to him, which he can only meet by creating maximum possible audiences for his own programs and "selling" those audiences to advertisers.

Thus, there is a logical and inevitable conflict between this requirement and the cable operator's potential function as a carrier of information for others. So long as the operator must reach maximum audiences, he is under a positive disincentive to foster programming of others to compete with his own program and dilute his audiences. Even though there are additional FCC rules affording various kinds of access by others to the operator's excess channels, the deck is variously stacked so these possibilities are not significant deterrents to the natural anticompetitive tendencies that flow from the operator's origination responsibilities.

By and large, the commission's approach would endow the operator with substantial power to foreclose major expansion in program access to subscribers by others than himself, so that essentially, the net benefit to the subscriber from the advent of cable television is the addition of only one more relatively weak channel. And herein lies the FCC's mischief, for in the 1970s the commission has only replicated its 1960s solution to the problem of oligopoly in the broadcast industry—when it freed a few more television channels by facilitating the growth of UHF stations.

In the process of rendering cable innocuous to the broadcasters, the FCC initiative tended to emasculate cable's ability to serve two relevant interest groups: consumers, whose rights to the fullest diversity of program services would be compromised; and potential programmers, who would find the cable operator standing in their way of gaining access through cable systems to consumers. In the process, what some might view as the FCC's highest responsibilities—to protect the public's Constitutional right to information under the First Amendment and, as an instrument of enforcement of the antitrust laws, to foster competition to the maximum extent possible—would have gone out the window.

Left to its own devices, the FCC would resolve questions about cable's future in the most retrograde fashion. Measured any way you like, that kind of future is a far cry from the development of cable as a broad and rich telecommunications highway that its enthusiasts anticipate lies just over the horizon.

Indeed, even the cable industry has not been much impressed by the ingenuity of mandatory origination. One can only assume that the start-up costs of building studios and operating a full schedule of local programming have proved more frightening than the long-range opportunities for regulatory shelter, given a basic lack of confidence the FCC could ever deliver enough compensations. One operator ungraciously (and unsuccessfully) challenged the commission's power in the Supreme Court, while others have mounted quieter (and more effective) efforts to keep the rule from being enforced, though it should be noted that a significant amount of origination does occur voluntarily.

Meanwhile, the key stone of the FCC's philosophical arch has never been put in place, and it is not clear what if any further strategems the commission might find to "get cable moving." Indeed, with economic pressures stalling the expansion of the industry, broadcasters have now mounted a powerful effort to roll it back, seeking tougher rules with respect to pay-cable, which they claim reduces the public's program choices over what is euphemistically called "free television"—for which, as previously noted, the public pays more than $4 billion in advertising costs this year.

Indeed, the cable industry is once more on the defensive, and the question of its future is just as unresolved now as ever.

## The Prospects for Consumer Leadership

To a very great extent, consumers retain the last word on cable development, or so all parties to the controversy appear to believe. For one thing, the mandatory origination rule was crafted with a view to making common cause between cable and public interest groups around the country. The ongoing pay-cable battle—lavishly funded with special warchests and so militantly waged for the public's benefit that cable interests are complaining at the FTC about unfair trade practices by the broadcasters—is targeted ultimately at persuading the TV viewer that there is (or is not) a plot to take away his sports and his reruns. Both interest groups believe if they can persuade consumers there is something to be gained or lost, their business objectives will be served. Congress will be impressed, and the FCC will click its heels.

Until relatively recently, consumer groups have not been particularly sophisticated in the use of their power, or even well informed that it exists.

There are, on the other hand, a couple of vital pressure points that are and ought to be fine targets for attention on the part of consumers, and are, fortunately, beginning to receive it.

The first is the organization of cable with respect to its message carriage and message generating functions. Sometimes, this is called the "common carrier" issue, by a misleading analogy to transportation and telephone services. By overdrawing the question (stimulating chilling fears of regulation of return on investment) opponents from the cable industry have tended to shout down its relevance. By imprecision in tailoring the concept to the subject matter, on the other hand, proponents played into the opposition's hands. Over the years, only the American Civil Liberties Union argued cogently that cable should be treated as a carrier, that is, a monopoly in *transmission* but a mechanism of free and open competition in *programming,* and its views were widely ignored.

Eventually, however, the "mandatory origination" rule drew enough informed interest that the carrier issue was more and more sharply focused. It became apparent that by a rule that would fuse cable's programming and transmission functions, the novel potential of cable for promoting diversity would be fatally perverted. A number of states began to realize their regulatory options would be foreclosed, and the Federal Communications Commission began to have second thoughts.

A most notable development occurred a few months ago when Consumers Union and United Church of Christ joined in urging the FCC to abandon the mandatory origination rule. Notable, in that this was the first entry into the cable field by the consumer movement's leading spokesman. Moreover, the filing was also remarkably pragmatic and nondoctrinaire for a so-called "public-interest" group. Recognizing that "infant industry" indulgences are appropriate for cable, the filing also urged the necessity of framing policies that offer the twin assurance that cable would grow and that it would grow in a pro-competitive fashion.

Significantly, so long as attention is rivetted on the broadcaster-cable conflict, federal regulation has been incapable of focusing sharply on required consumer protections (both for consumers directly and indirectly through protecting competition among programmers who may well include consumers groups themselves). Even the present White House cable bill—that has yet to make it through the bureaucratic clearance process and may never get to Capitol Hill—ignores the essentiality of assurance that cable will survive its adolescence and fulfill its promises.

In another, complementary area—the financing of cable development—consumer groups are beginning to make their considerable weight felt. Heavy capital requirements have been the broadcasters' major chokepoints over cable, and the cable industry's major argument to avoid effective regulation. As speculative investments, cable systems find capital dear and regulatory imposition of service burdens onerous. But if systems were mature and recognized as stable utilities, the cost of capital would come down and the availability of capital would increase.

Consumers can break this cycle of dependence by backing public policies to make long-term, low-interest funds available to cable systems operating in the public interest. Be it through loans, pledges of credit, or even tax revenues, service-oriented cable systems have justifiable claims upon public funds—claims quite as good as interstate highways. Even assuming that public ownership is undesirable where transmission of information is involved—actually a questionable premise if transmission and programming functions are split—government involvement in the process of capital formation is highly justified, given the enormous social and economic benefits anticipated from cable systems.

In a number of areas, municipal bonding is being considered for cable facilities. Moreover, growing attention is being given to the role of cooperatives in cable development. An effort is now getting underway to pry open low-interest Rural Electrification Administration loan funds for rural cooperatives, for areas where both the needs and costs of wiring may be greatest. If such an effort can get underway—Congress' Office of Technology Assessment is beginning a study, under prodding from various elements of the consumer and cooperative movements—a highly compelling precedent can be launched for cable development generally.

Thus, consumers groups are at long last now making their weight felt— selectively and perceptively—in the two areas—organization and finance—that have the biggest future payoff in shaping cable television development. My own view is that *only* a substantial effort to influence public policy—both in terms of regulation and developmental programs—will make very much of cable's promise mature very soon.


### Consumer Leadership, Business Opportunity

What does the cable industry think of all this? Five years ago, cable operators would dismiss such talk as madness, or, to use one of their favorite expressions, pie in the sky. Today, they are not quite so sure of the wisdom or the prac- ticality of keeping consumerism down. For although the thrust of consumerism is to protect consumers against cable operators, cable's entry into communica- tions markets and its legitimacy vis-à-vis broadcasters would also be assured. All those public-service burdens seem to have their rewards as well, and cable operators, no less than any other businessmen, are very concerned about where and how they will spend eternity.

When the public was more or less indifferent to cable, consumers, like the pope, had zero divisions. With cable on the defensive and consumers aroused, the prospects of a true partnership are becoming more real. That day may not be here yet, but at least the perceptions of each other's existence and needs are now growing all the sharper.

Our consideration of "consumer activism and business interests in cable tele- vision development" ought to be viewed as more than just a special case of a regulated, infant industry straining for market entry. Industry by industry, the players and the prices may differ, but I submit, the rule remains the same:

That is, a truly informed and alert consumer movement can and should take the lead to define market opportunities for business, rewarding good performance with sales and loyalty and keeping scoundrels *out*. Businesses should appreciate that their best partners are their customers. With a perception of such common interest, the relationship between the two need not be one of eternal dismay.


### Note

1. Arthur R. Burns, *The Decline of Competition* (New York, McGraw-Hill, Inc., 1936), p. 574.

# Discussion

*Question:* What about political control and whether the system of broad band communication has more dangers to society than benefits?

*Rivkin:* I suggest that the question is seldom posed so fundamentally. The pursuit of cable television has to be accomplished on somewhat elitist principles. That is, one senses that it is a good idea and pursues the idea. Cable television is inevitable. Furthermore, it ought to be built because the costs of not building such systems are too high.

*Question:* What about the threat to broadcasting from cable television?

*Rivkin:* I think the consumers and public interest groups must recognize no one is ever going to drive broadcasting out of business. That being the case, the question is how do you co-exist between cable and broadcasting? How do you define an appropriate future for broadcasting that also recognizes and fosters the many and desirable advantages of two-way communication via cable. That does take a certain amount of regulatory initiative. It requires that people acknowledge that broadcasters will be around for quite a while. It requires a deliberate policy to put as much of the United States as possible on cable and to establish three or four or five channels of mass television, which will be the existing broadcasters in any market. It requires the development of the capital base. And the sooner the infrastructure of cable reaching into everyone's home and business can be created, the easier the transition is going to be.

*Comment:* You are offering us a very peculiar problem. In the normal situation, industry develops the product and if the product is successful the product acquires consumers. The problems most of us have dealt with in the past. involve consumers realizing, for example, that the products they are dependent on are not safe or possibly have additives in them. Then regulatory problems arise. How do you regulate products that are already being produced? The problem you are offering us is a different one. In a sense you are saying that industry has not produced the product yet for various reasons; it is not available. As a result, there are no consumers of cable television, at least of all the services you've projected. Yet you are asking consumers to join the cable industry in a push to obtain cable. There is no organized consumer group for it because most people are not even aware of its existence. As an organizational problem, it is very difficult to organize consumers that don't exist. Moreover, one additional problem: Even if you could get over that hurdle, it's not clear, I would suspect, that they would know what they are getting into. The first question is, do we really want cable? We don't know because we don't have the product yet; we don't have any experience with it. So it's a very peculiar kind of consumer problem.

*Rivkin:* What are the mechanisms by which the consumer movement may function to accomplish its basic objectives. There are large ranges of human activities with which consumers are concerned and which impose costs upon people and burdens, and they are not accomplished as efficiently as they might be through communications technology. Rational land use and economic development is one. The accomplishment of educational services is another. Delivery of health services is a third. A whole range of things go far beyond the communications issue in itself but wherein communications technology appears to be relevant. If society is sufficiently concerned about solving those basic underlying problems it will necessarily emphasize the development of communications systems as a desirable tool to accomplish them. In terms of communication policy alone it doesn't seem to me cable is very justified. In terms of a social commitment to doing a range of things for which cable is relevant, there is the tremendous social interest in insuring that this technology is fully developed to enable it to make whatever contribution it can.

# 5

## Warranties: A Study of Marketplace Reactions in the Automobile Industry

### John C. Secrest

The matter of consumerism, with all of its implications, is something business leaders must face squarely—not for altruistic reasons, but because the well-being of our companies and our competitive enterprise system depends on it.

There has been much discussion and debate, and businessmen obviously are concerned. Yet, this concern has not been fully reflected in the marketplace—which is where it counts.

The fundamental management issue is expressed by a venerable idea about the competitive market, one which has existed since the beginning of commerce. That is, if business treats customers fairly, customers treat business fairly. It sounds like an old cliché, but realistically implemented, it works.

In our complex world, it is possible to lose sight of what customer satisfaction really means, to do only what is necessary, rather than what good business judgement tells us is right. Business, to succeed and grow, sells and promotes what is new and better. We need a broader concept of these words—one which from a pragmatic management standpoint recognizes that competition for consumer loyalty and support, and consequently for sales and profits, is now just as real after the sale as it is before the sale is made.

We know that today consumer confidence in industry is falling. This is not an invention of critics; it is a fact of life and something must be done about it. Management attitudes about accepting responsibility for product problems or defects are an important key to remedying this.

We are playing for high stakes. The stakes are political, as well as economic. Dissatisfaction with product performance and service means more than lost business. It primarily explains why people have not more seriously questioned the cost or effect of wide-ranging regulation by government.

Some rules and guidelines established by government are desirable—and necessary—but not if regulation extends to encompass the whole range of market-related decisions, so these areas are controlled in large degree by government regulation rather than by business. We have already seen that this is costly and inefficient, and that, in practice, consumer legislation usually does not produce the benefits it promises. But more fundamentally, the very success of our system depends upon the freedom and the ability of industry to make decisions based upon competitive realities. This, after all, is where our principal skills are focused, and where experience has clearly indicated that government's skills are least effective.

For the future, we can be sure that expectations of consumers will continue to rise—probably even more rapidly than in the past, while their impatience with problems of quality and service will intensify. In these circumstances, overreliance on government will surely lead only to more frustration and disillusionment.

Nevertheless, the hard core consumerists will continue to press for legislative actions in the name of the consumer, and unless business adopts a strong, positive posture, some of these actions will be taken. Once taken, they will tend to be locked in concrete—whether or not they are necessary or economically sound, and whether or not their effect is to impinge on the consumer's freedom of choice in a competitive marketplace.

The point to emphasize is that there already is a vast web of existing laws and government agencies in the area of consumer protection. On the federal level alone, a recent count indicated approximately five dozen agencies administering 1,000 consumer programs at an annual cost of $3 billion. A good case can be made that a real problem in this respect already is the gross wastefulness and inefficiency of pyramiding duplication—and that what is needed is not more regulation created in an atmosphere of expediency, but an intelligent assessment of powers that already exist.

More than this, the whole atmosphere of the marketplace has changed. The consumer is king, not for idealistic reasons,but for a specific, visible reason—his buying power, much of which is discretionary. His decisions to buy or not to buy have a tremendous effect upon the operation of businesses.

These sum up the realities on which any business or industry must base a useful strategy for meeting the challenge of consumerism. They say to us clearly that traditional marketing or publicity programs, however well-meaning, will not be enough; that what business does not do voluntarily will likely sooner or later become mandatory; that the cost of an aggressive consumer-oriented strategy could be vastly less than the ultimate cost in the marketplace of poor performance by business—or the appearance of poor performance.

In this respect, we at American Motors believe our Buyer Protection Plan has some useful things to say about how a plan of action can be put to work in the marketplace. In developing the plan, we faced some basic facts about the auto industry, which apply generally to all industries.

One fact is that no matter what is done on production lines, or how much money is spent on quality control procedures, the auto industry is never going to achieve a completely defect-free car. It is not a practical possibility. We have found that people do not expect a completely defect free car—but they do expect, rightfully, that problems which occur will be fixed rapidly and without unnecessary cost or inconvenience. The trouble is that many car buyers feel—and our research studies showed this—that once the car is theirs, no one really cares about their problems. Genuine efforts throughout the auto industry—better warranties, service training programs, quality control emphasis—have not been enough. Car buyers expect more of our industry than they have been getting.

Another fact that came through very clearly is that manufacturers and dealers must jointly overcome uncertainties that cause customer dissatisfaction. Dealers have too often been caught in the middle between factory and customer. When problems arose, one all-inportant question sometimes remained— and that was who would pay the bill: the factory, the dealer, or the customer? There was a large gray area. The good dealers—and there are many good ones for every bad one—wanted to favor the customer. A lot of costs were absorbed, but sometimes they were not. The customer wound up with the bill, and he did not like it.

We looked at these facts, and frankly we considered ways to meet them that might minimize the risk—the possible cost exposure. But we decided there was only one way to do it, that is, to stand 100 percent behind our products, and eliminate all questions about cost of guarantee repairs and of predelivery service at the dealership. We accepted these costs as a factory responsibility and a factory responsibility only. Our concept of the Buyer Protection Plan is to pay for everything for which we are responsible, plus anything else where it makes good business sense to give the benefit of the doubt to the dealer and customer. This has been the key to the success of the Buyer Protection Plan. It has, very simply, given our dealers full incentive to emphasize service in the same way they emphasize sales.

By and large, our dealers have done just that—and without this response, the plan would never have worked. When we first talked with our dealers and our employees about the plan, we said it was not only a marketing programs but an integrated design, manufacturing, and financial plan woven into the fabric of our company as a long-range commitment to a new way of life.

This is what it takes to overcome the cynicism and doubt that obviously surrounded the subject of warranties—in the auto industry and elsewhere. We have not just accepted increased sales and earnings as proof to us that our concept is effective. Through our nationwide hot line, checks by field sales personnel and direct customer surveys, we have monitored how well we are doing. We have found that car buyers believe we are keeping our promise. Significantly, independent surveys conducted outside the auto industry show the same thing.

In each of the past two years Boston College has surveyed new car buyers on warranty satisfaction. In the 1974 study, we rated far above other makes, with 89 percent of our owners reporting definite satisfaction with their warranties. The next highest make recorded 77 percent.

The study went on to show a definite correlation between customer satisfaction with warranties and purchase decisions. Again, American Motors was far ahead, with 68 percent of our buyers saying warranty protection was very or extremely important in their choice of an AMC car. The next make has 42 percent.

There is another recent indication of how we are doing—in the issue of the *Harvard Business Review* (September-October, 1974, p. 58). A survey of the publication's subscribers included a question on which companies are doing an effective job responding to consumer pressures. American Motors led the way, with over 20 percent of the respondents mentioning us. That is more than eight percentage points above any of the other 14 firms cited.

These survey results have been confirmed in the marketplace—demonstrating graphically that this plan is not altruism—but good business.

The plan unquestionably has contributed to the sales momentum American Motors is enjoying. In the several months prior to initiating our Buyer Protection Plan in 1972, we were taking 2.7 percent of the domestic passenger car market. With no major product change the next year, we realized 3.3 percent market penetration, a 22 percent gain. In 1973 our market share rose to 3.8 percent. This year our share of market is 4.7 percent, a 75 percent gain over 1971. While not the only reason for this continuing corporate progress, the Buyer Protection Plan has certainly been a major factor.

For compelling reasons, the Buyer Protection Plan is part of American Motors and its way of doing business. We believe that it will enable us to earn and deserve recognition increasingly as a company that cares about people.

To summarize, in the process of growing rapidly, business has helped to create pressures of change and rising expectations, and hindsight now tell us that we did not define and react to these trends as well as we should have.

I believe most progressive business leaders recognize the need to adjust to these new consumer attitudes—and there is tangible evidence of this in changes taking place at the point of sale and after the sale.

Doing something about it requires an effort stretching from executive offices to salesrooms. Problems of consumerism are not factory problems or dealer problems, but common problems, and, emphatically, management problems—for management must set the tone for resolution.

I am confident that American business has the capability to meet the challenge of growing consumer sophistication and expectations, and can do so without more regulation. It is a challenge to change entrenched attitudes and practices of many years standing, but our experience with the Buyer Protection Plan proves it can be done—and with gratifying results.

# 6

## Warranties: A Study of Marketplace Reactions in the Appliance Industry

*Daniel J. Krumm*

At one time it was not uncommon to find business and industry leaders suggesting that "consumerism" was just a phase that would soon pass away like a number of other temporarily annoying situations. Fortunately, that has not been the case. In all levels within the business community, there is a growing awareness that customer concerns are our concerns. The consumer movement has gone a long way in placing the proper emphasis on product quality and service, and manufactures have responded to this need.

It would be well for us to recall the development of the appliance industry in the past few decades.

The traditional major appliance—the refrigerator with the compressor on the top, the washer that featured the latest balloon-type wringer-rolls—had very few things that could go wrong. When they did break down, which was seldom, the problem could often be remedied with a good kick in the right spot, usually from mama. The warranty that accompanied such an appliance was an official-looking legal document, seldom referred to. Today's appliances are far more sophisticated, and it also takes a little more mechanical ability that can be found in the foot to keep them running. At the same time, today's appliances are truly better values than the ones purchased in the "good old days."

Appliance industry statistics show that the frequency of repair on automatic washers in warranty has declined by three-fourths since 1959. There has also been a two-thirds decline in service required on electrical clothes dryers during that same period. These are not only better products, they are less expensive as well. The appliance industry has established a rather remarkable record in the face of general price trends. Since 1959, the consumer price index has risen 53 percent, while appliance prices represented in that index have fallen about 8 percent.

If appliances are better values today, one might ask why the voice of critics has become so much louder. In addition to the consumer movement, there are other good reasons for this: The total number of appliances in each home has grown so rapidly in the past decade that, in spite of the reduced frequency of breakdown per individual appliance, the aggregate repair problem has grown larger. Also, today's busy housewife has become much more dependent upon her home appliance products. Finally, consumers, in general, are far less patient than they were a few years back. Although they once were willing to wait a few days for service, this is no longer acceptable to them. When an appliance breaks down today, the housewife both expects and demands immediate solutions to her problems.

If you were to purchase a Maytag washer today, it would be exactly the same as the one your neighbor purchased in 1966—the last time we made a major change in our line. While this washer may look the same, however, there have been roughly 500 specification changes in the product during those eight years.

Maytag has never followed the practice of introducing new models. In recent years other companies in our industry have also turned away from introducing a new line every time the calendar turns. The result is that appliance manufacturers who don't have to retool production lines and retrain employees every year have the time to concentrate their efforts on building better products. Yet, there is a need for consumer protection legislation in the product service area of the appliance industry.

In 1969, when everyone was taking a harder look at their policies, after the president's task force on product safety was formed, most appliance manufacturers made several changes in their warranties. Maytag, for instance, changed the formal language and format of its warranties, to make them more understandable and meaningful to the consumer. Maytag also added protection for the consumer who moves out of his selling dealer's area while his product is still in warranty. We made a number of other changes, and so did other manufacturers in our industry who represent about 95 percent of all major appliances sold.

It is therefore difficult to accept the conclusion made in a House subcommittee report, which stated that, in spite of the task force's recommendations, product warranties "often are frauds protecting the manufacturer or seller more than the buyer."[1] The report also lists the 11 types of exemptions that manufacturers use in their warranties to escape obligations. The only exemption they found in Maytag's warranty was that we warrant our consumer products "for home use only." For a variety of reasons, including the safety of the operator, we feel it is in the consumer's best interest to use our home laundry equipment to do the family wash. We do market another appliance for commercial use, and the warranty on this appliance so states.

Several other major manufacturers were cited for requiring that the consumer return the warranty card. Although Maytag does not have this in its warranty, there may be a very good reason why other manufacturers do. The National Product Safety Act requires that manufacturers be able to identify users of their products; yet the act does not hold either the consumer or the dealer responsible for providing this information to the company. One of the few ways the manufacturer has open to him to get such information is to have the consumer return the warranty card.

Maytag supports the federal legislation for federal regulation of consumer product warranties in its amended form, but even this bill—actually there are two, but both accomplish about the same thing—has some consumer drawbacks.

One of the complaints made by the House subcommittee was that warranties were too long and the language was too complicated. This new legislation specifically spells out what the content of a warranty must be. It states that the manufacturer must tell whether the warranty is full or limited, who the person is making the warranty, what the consumer must do to secure fulfillment of the warranty, what expenses the consumer might incur, and what legal remedies are available to him.

Well, you can bet that the manufacturer's legal department is going to get involved in writing such a warranty. It is my opinion that such a bill will tend to nullify any progress that has been made to date in simplifying the language of warranties. We will once again find many warranties that will require the services of a trained lawyer to interpret them, and certainly that is not the goal of the ethical manufacturer, nor is it the goal of the consumer movement.

There are a number of state bills now pending that say if a dealer is required to fulfill part of the warranty, the manufacturer must reimburse him to do so. On the surface, this would appear to be a logical requirement. Most manufacturers have accepted it, and now are applying the policy throughout the country, even though it is required in only two states. In fact, Maytag is virtually alone in opposing such legislation. We think our position is justified in the name of good consumerism. For a manufacturer to set up an escrow account to which it can charge such costs requires substantial administrative overhead. A staff is required to process claims, write checks, verify service, etc. A manufacturer will estimate the cost of providing the in-warranty service by using a formula that will protect him from dealer inefficiencies. All of these costs will be passed along to the consumer in the form of higher prices. Under our present arrangement, the dealer provides the labor for in-warranty service. He, of course, includes such costs in his price to the consumer. The difference, however, is that an efficient dealer can provide such service at a much lower cost per unit than a manufacturer must charge. The dealer is concerned only with his own operation, not with a retailer 2,000 miles away whose service department may not be as efficient as his. He knows that the lower he can hold his retail prices, the more competitive he will be. He has the incentive to provide efficient, in-warranty service because this is one area over which he has some control. When the manufacturer begins to pick up the tab for the labor involved, however, the dealer no longer has the same reason for holding down these costs.

In the two states—California and Minnesota—where we have had experience with such laws, our more efficient dealers do not like it. They tell us they had been providing the same service for about half the price we have found it necessary to add to our wholesale prices in order to comply with the laws. When we established these rates, we attempted to make them as realistic as possible—we did not expect to derive a profit. Our goal was more than met. At the end of July, we were running in the red in providing in-warranty service in every product category in California—the only state where we have had enough experience to make a meaningful study.

The greatest benefit that has come from the emphasis on warranties is that the consumer has discovered the importance of quality service after the sale. It was not too many years ago when a common sales pitch was, "I can give you x dollars off if you take it without service." Those in the industry who were concerned with consumer satisfaction were disturbed by the success of that approach. It proved beyond doubt that many consumers would respond more favorably to a low price than to quality service. We used to discuss the need for consumer education in this area but, in spite of our efforts, we recognized that such education, to be effective, would have to come from other sources more clearly identified with consumer interests. The consumerism movement has gone a long way to accomplish this. People talk good service more than in the past, and with more apparent sincerity and conviction. Quality after-sale service has become as much a product feature as the lint filter on a dryer. Also, manufacturers who were not as concerned with product dependability began to upgrade the quality of their products. They discovered that today's better-educated, more vocal consumers insisted that more attention be directed to quality, and this concern was reflected in their buying habits. The escalating cost of providing in-warranty service also was an incentive for manufacturers to increase quality control at the factory.

The growing awareness by consumers of the value of good service has resulted in manufacturers responding in a number of different ways. Maytag was a step ahead of its competition in recognizing the need. We introduced a service program in 1961 aimed at providing the good quality appliance service that today's homemaker demands and deserves. Maytag's Red Carpet Service now is available in every major city through the United States and to some 70 percent of the population. This program offers speedy and efficient response to a plea for appliance service, plus personal attention to detail appreciated by all homemakers. Any Maytag servicing dealer who is capable of adhering to the high standards set forth in the program is eligible to become a licensed Maytag Red Carpet Service dealer.

A Red Carpet Service license requires that service be provided within 24 hours of the time the customer calls. Servicemen must be factory trained, and are required to wear a standard uniform. The service vehicle must carry a complete stock of repair parts. Each serviceman is equipped with two red carpets. One carpet is placed on the floor and the other is used to protect the appliance itself. The serviceman polishes the appliance after it is repaired, leaving it as clean or cleaner than he found it. When he is finished, he gives the customer a chance to evaluate his efforts. A postage-paid report card gives the dealer the opportunity to keep a close check on the quality of service being performed. Other firms have started similar programs—many in response to the consumer movement.

One of the things we learned when looking at our service programs nationally was that approximately 30 percent of all service calls—both in and out of warranty--were unnecessary. Had the consumer read the instruction book or made a few quick checks, it would have saved a service call. One leading magazine estimates that some $80 million is wasted annually on unnecessary service calls. We began to ask ourselves why this was happening, and we learned it was not all the fault of the consumer. For at least the past 30 years, the instruction books for Maytag appliances have been prepared with the help and advice of our home economists, our product testing engineers, and our marketing supervisors. Quite frankly, we thought we were doing an excellent job. But were we really? One of the side effects of the widespread interest in consumerism has been that many people who would not previously have written directly to a manufacturer now feel almost compelled to do so. We became aware that our communications were not quite as effective as we had supposed. Now these two examples certainly are not typical, but I would like to relate them to you to illustrate my point.

One woman sent us a bundle of her laundry to prove that her washer was literally eating up her clothes. We felt the damage was the result of an indiscriminate use of bleach and were startled when she quite bluntly informed us she never in her life used bleach—she always used Clorox! Another woman sent us samples of her laundry and told us her washer simply was not getting her clothes clean. One look was all we needed to agree with her completely. But when we washed them in our own laboratory using standard practices, they came out sparkling white. A little face-to-face discussion between the housewife and one of our home economists revealed she was not using any soap, detergent, or any other laundering aid: She had bought an automatic washer hadn't she? Surely she didn't have to put soap or detergent in it, or how could we call it automatic? Those two letters helped convince us our instruction books may not be as easy to understand as we had thought—particularly for those who may not be literate in English.

In 1969 Maytag assigned two college marketing instructors to research the problem. They tested a proposed set of simplified instructions with women undergoing homemaking training in a manpower development training project in New York City. The study confirmed our suspicion. Recommendations as a result of this study included the use of many more illustrations, fewer words, and simpler language. For example, soiled garments should be referred to as dirty clothes. Illustrations should show the desired action actually and clearly being done; it is not enough just to show the appliance part or control by itself. The study indicated that many persons will prefer to follow the action shown in illustrations, rather than read the text. As a result of the study, all operating instructions of Maytag appliances have been revised to conform to the simplifications recommended. Additionally, Maytag continues to cooperate with academic research projects designed to improve the clarity and effectiveness of written instructions. Maytag instruction manuals are reviewed annually.

No segment of the economy has more interest in the needs of the consumer than the appliance industry. An example of this awareness is the establishment of MACAP—Major Appliance Consumer Action Panel—by the Association of

Home Appliance Manufacturers. This independent consumer watchdog committee, which includes experts not employed in the major appliance industry, has acted effectively and responsibly in settling over 80 percent of the consumer complaints it has received. Such well-known consumer advocates as Virginia Knauer have publicly noted MACAP's progress, and several other industries are now establishing similar organizations. MACAP has been cited by the highest consumer agencies as an outstanding example of self-regulation in an industry. Two years ago, it earned the Abby award from the National Council of Better Business Bureaus for its performance. If a consumer has a problem with an appliance that cannot be resolved through her local dealer, or with the manufacturer, MACAP studies the complaint and makes a recommendation for an equitable solution.

Somehow a lengthy warranty implies to the consumer that it is a quality product — the longer the warranty, the better the appliance. Quite frankly, this is simply not the case. Some manufacturers look upon a warranty as a sales tool. As often as not, the person who writes the warranty on the product at such a firm is assigned to the marketing division rather than to manufacturing or research where quality is designed and produced.

A retailer at a seminar recently asked us why our food waste disposer, which he felt was a better product than that of another make, carried only a two-year warranty, while another brand was warranted for five years. Another dealer attending the seminar pointed out that the manufacturer of the other brand also warranted his disposer for two years, but that the distributor in the area had simply tacked on another three years. No distributor, of course, controls the quality of a manufacturer's product, nor is he going to go out on a limb and protect it free for an extra three years. He's going to add the cost of this protection, based on his experience, to the amount he charges for the unit. To many consumers, however, the five-year warranty would indicate they were buying a product of superior quality to that of another make that carries only a two-year warranty. But the product with the five-year warranty might well wear out long before one with a shorter warranty. Perhaps a consumer who is dealing with an unknown manufacturer is afforded some type of added protection from a longer warranty, but it is in the consumer's best interest to deal with a reputable firm — a firm that knows it is in its own best interest, indeed imperative to its survival, that the product it manufactures is designed and produced to provide consumer satisfaction.

We always have believed in consumerism at Maytag, although we have not always called it that. For instance, we provide functional repair parts for every product we made, for so long as there is any demand — and then some, to make sure. We still stock and occasionally sell parts for wringer washers made before I was born. We recently formalized this practice into a policy statement, signifying the intent to provide any repair part or interchangeable substitute for a period of 25 years from the date of last production using said part. To us, consumerism is doing the best job possible to serve our customers well. We welcome the rediscovery of quality of product, because so long as we remain quality oriented, we cannot help but benefit from the trend.

It is not my intent to cast other companies is an unfavorable light by reviewing Maytag's philosophy and policies. I confess to believing that Maytag is a cut above the average in these respects, but I can only speak knowledgeably about Maytag. I sincerely believe the differences between Maytag and other successful companies are more a matter of degree and method than a matter of substance. I am convinced that most companies that are consistently successful apply sound business ethics when responding to consumer needs—whether or not the customer is protected by a warranty.

## Note

1. Subcommittee on Commerce and Finance of the House Interstate and Foreign Commerce Committee, September 17, 1974.

# Discussion

*Comment:* One auto manufacturer, in a filing a few months ago with the U.S. Department of Transportation, opposed gasoline tank rupture protection in crashes because it would cost $11 or $12 dollars, if I remember the figures per car, to save an unfortunately low figure of 180 people from burning to death in overturning crashes each year. In opposing that federal proposal, it totally failed to mention any or at least certain of the pertinent externalities—the spill over cost, to give you one. There was no mention in that proposal, which proported to be a cost-benefit analysis of the cost to the public of the huge amount of activity on the part of the fire departments in responding to fuel spillages, actual fires, and threats of fires, involving vehicles on the roads. The Insurance Institute for Highway Safety decided to look at this. They hired a reputable economic research firm and discovered the best estimate that could be made of this cost annually in the United States alone was $350 million. When one put that figure into the equation one got a completely different answer.

*Question:* Do firms enforce standards?

*Krumm:* Manufacturers' interests and the dealers' interests may be different. We have about 10,000 Maytag dealers throughout the United States, out of a total of 40,000 appliance dealers. When their interest is not the same as ours, how do we enforce standards? We have no dealer who is not licensed. A license is reissued to him each year and each dealer is called upon by an emloyee of the Maytag company to review the requirements and standards of the license. There is still a second agreement for a dealer who meets very high service standards to be a Red Carpet Service dealer. Some dealers may have both of these or they may have only one. But these are reviewed annually. However, I should emphasize that we don't just cancel a license without good reason. The dealer and the company both have rights under the agreement. You first select dealers with great care. You try to train them as well as you possibly can and before you decide not to reissue a license you try to get them to fulfill their obligations under the agreement. You consider cancellation only when they flagrantly are in violation of your license.

You might wonder why we don't control our dealers. If you stop and think, there is a tremendous amount of competition that goes on on the sales floor of the dealer because most dealers carry many lines, not just Maytag, and we're just one among them. The way they sell Maytag is often significantly different, interestingly enough, from other products, because we have a distinctive product that cannot be successfully sold by some traditional methods. It is a constant challenge to maintain the selling force you need from that dealer that he may not be required to give for another manufacturer. I think we are the only appliance manufacturer in the continental United States who deals directly with nearly every one of our dealers except for one distributor in Boston. Most companies deal through distributors. A Maytag employee calls on every one of these 10,000 dealers. We do have a core of dealers, called Maytag Home Appliance Centers, that have chosen to be exclusive Maytag stores. They are not owned by the Maytag Company but they have been set up under a concept basis and there you have vastly more cooperation because Maytag is what they've committed themselves to and they are very fine operations.

How do we absorb these additional costs or do we absorb them or do we pass them on? It's thoroughly obvious from what I said to you about what's happened to appliance pricing. They have been absorbed to a large extent and the industry has found ways to trim costs and yet come up with a better product. In 1974 we celebrated the 25th anniversary of the manufacture of the first Maytag automatic washer. Prior to 1949 all we made was the wringer washer. We were the last people, I think, to get into the business. To celebrate this event we decided to look for the oldest Maytag automatic washer still operating and found it in Story City, Iowa. It was the twelfth automatic washer we ever made and interestingly enough the owner paid about the same amount for that washing machine as she could buy one for today, which explains what we've done with costs through the years. A lot have been designed out of the product, obviously. Today's product is infinitely better than the one bought 25 years ago. But costs of all appliances are going up significantly. Whenever you have sudden cost increases, you don't have time to absorb them. They have to be passed on. I don't know that this is totally bad. Maybe appliances have been underpriced.

*Secrest:* Do we pass on the price of the buyer protection plan to the public? American Motors had done quite a bit of research with its own people and had an outside consulting firm do research into what really bothered consumers when it came to owning cars and purchasing cars. We determined there was a very strong feeling on the part of the consumers that the quality of the cars wasn't what it used to be, that there were too many things that went wrong with the cars, and that when they went wrong there was too much hassle and too much cost to the consumer in paying for it, particuarly in the early years. When we digested all of this, it wasn't new but it just came to us as input because we were looking for a major program to give importance to our company and to become a stronger competitor and more profitable in the business. Although we didn't realize we were going to spend many millions of dollars on this program, we knew we couldn't charge one penny more for our products. When it came to pricing the 1972 cars, we had to price against Ford and General Motors and Chrysler, and we did price right on them. In fact our Gremlin usually has been priced under everyone else, or else priced on them. So we knew we had a good many millions of dollars to absorb in this and we were doing it, for we felt it would be meaningful to the customers, that we would substantially increase our sales by doing it, that our dealers would become enthusiastic about it and push the sales, and that we would attract new dealers. All of these things materialized; so we did it for these reasons and there's no way to make a cost pass through.

I'm not against altruism. We are not cold blooded people. We would rather have happy customers and we would rather have happy dealers. You don't have to be a do-gooder if you can ascertain real, definable customer needs and pinpoint what they really are and not get off on tangent areas where it doesn't hit the mark. We think it can be good business for companies to do this, and also profitable; as a result you live up to your social responsibilities and things that you would like to do for people.

*Krumm:* In regard to providing *meaningful* performance information, when you are talking about a washing machine one of the things you want to know is how much it holds, how much water it uses, how much electricity it uses and these kinds of things. There is a real trend in the industry towards this. We've done a great deal of study of it and the American Home Appliance Manufacturers Association has a committee on standards that has spent a tremendous amount of time in recent months trying to find some meaningful way for the industry to approach it. This is something we're coming to. However, the industry has to approach it as a whole. Products are so different and if you can't get a common denominator so you can really compare the performance that we say Maytag has to what General Electric has on a comparable model, it doesn't really mean anything to you. We do provide all kinds of performance information on Maytag, but how do you relate that to someone else's performance? This is an industry-wide job. There is work that can be done there and should be done.

# 7

## A New Standard for Business: Positive Participation in the Legislative Process

*Peter T. Jones*

There is a new standard to which business must repair if we, as a society, are to survive and progress in the coming decades. Some call it a new dimension to corporate social responsibility; others call it a new enlightened self-interest; still others call it a new prescription for sheer survival. In reality, it is all three.

What is this standard? It is a positive participation in the legislative process, rather than negative opposition to the legislative process. No longer will negative business opposition to virtually every consumer proposition suffice — thus, one reason for our initial and continued support for the Consumer Protection Agency bill. But a decent respect for the opinions of mankind and especially of those in business who, while shrinking in number, still oppose both the general thesis of positive participation in the legislative arena and the specific proposal for a new Consumer Protection Agency (CPA), requires us to explain our reasons for so believing.

We hold ten truths to be self-evident, ten truths that argue for both the general and the specific views advanced here.

First, if business truly believes that the consumer always comes first, and states this publicly, it makes no sense always to oppose whatever consumers, or their representatives, propose.

Second, although we are providing the American public with one of the more efficient, responsible, and protective marketing systems in the world, we believe it can be further improved, for example: flammable pajamas, gas guzzling cars, faulty cribs, dangerous drugs, fraud on land sales, etc.

Third, many Americans today feel alienated, frustrated, and powerless in the face of forces beyond their control. Consumers who do not feel suspicious of business and government, who do not feel shut out and unrepresented in government proceedings that affect their pocketbooks, their well being, and the quality of their lives will be better customers of ours, and of other businesses that are, in fact, trying to serve them well. We believe the selective support of consumer proposals including the creation of a new Consumer Protection Agency, as an advocate for consumer interests in government, will contribute to consumer trust, and ultimately to better economic results for consumers and business alike.

Fourth, either the businessman will help lead in the arena of social change or someone else will. The businessman who stays out will have no one to blame but himself if the solutions offered are not workable. Within his competencies, the businessman should become a prime mover for change at the rule-making

59

level, whether in national, stage, or local government. He should not fight to preserve the status quo. There are plenty of others who will do that for him. He must fight for constructive changes that will apply to all companies in his industry.

Fifth, all too often businessmen and their trade association representatives appear at hearings in a totally defensive posture, saying, "You can't do this to us." Businessmen must take a new attitude. It is a matter of appearing at the hearing, and saying, "You *must* do this to us, this is what it will cost, what is technically feasible, and this is what the result will be, in terms of better products, better service, better air and better water."

Sixth, business has in many ways been its own worst enemy in the eyes of the American public. Since the nineteenth century, business has had an almost unbroken record of all-out opposition to legislation that the public thinks is good. The Sherman Anti-Trust Act, the Federal Reserve Act, the Federal Trade Commission Act, the Securities Exchange Act: we fought every one of them and lost. The Child Labor Act, The Federal Housing Act, The Federal Education Act, The Poverty Program and Medicare: all the same story — business opposing, trying to hold back the clock, and the legislation passing anyway.

Seventh, there can be no one today who feels *all* this legislation was bad for business. It has become the environment in which business as a whole has thrived and enjoyed unprecedented prosperity and vitality. The thoughtful businessman today agrees that, for the most part, this pattern of legislation has updated our free enterprise system, made it still more viable under today's worldwide conditions of rapid change, and has thus contributed to the good of all of society, including business.

Eight, unfortunately business leadership did not see it that way as it was happening. They behaved in a paradoxical way, absolutely contrary to the way they handle their own business affairs. Forward looking and adaptable to change in running our own business, they fought for the status quo when considering legislative solutions to social needs and problems.

Ninth, many polls in recent years show a sinking of public trust and confidence in our major institutions, including government, labor, and business. Inflation, stagflation, recession, rising gas and food prices, and declining employment all contribute to this current lack of confidence. This decline in the public regard for business is not something we can take lightly. A growing number of citizens believe that businessmen are apt to be dishonest, are making money by deception, monopoly, or conspiracy. For the first time in decades a growing number of these same people are beginning to question the fundamentals of our economic system, for all its vaunted efficiency, beginning to think that its aims and/or functioning may be in conflict with the needs and interests of the people it serves. Instant negative opposition by business in the legislative arena contributes to this questioning.

Tenth, and most important, if our free enterprise system is itself being called into question, then everyone is in real trouble. This thing called private competitive, free enterprise, is basically a notion of decentralized economic decision making. That is a synonym for decentralized economic power, which is a principal safeguard any society needs to preserve decentralized political power, the essence of democracy. If all the economic power is in the hands of a few, right or left, public or private, sooner or later they will get all the political power, too. Then instead of living our lives on a voluntary basis, we will live our lives on a basis of coercion by the minority, the essence of dictatorship.

From these ten self-evident truths, is it not also self-evident that we all have a common cause in business becoming more positive in its participation, more socially responsible in its role, in the legislative arena? How do we accomplish this? We cannot continue to have virtually every major corporation in the country lining up in solid phalanx on the hillside firing mortar shots of "no's" down onto the plain, just trying to preserve the status quo. Business must get down on the legislative plain, grapple with the issues, and work out the necessary compromises. Periodically this will require business publicly to support proposals not fully to our liking – as the price we must pay to avoid something still less to our liking.

The problem is, there is a universal herd instinct in all of us to huddle together against change. There is nothing more threatening than to have one member of the herd pull out and go it alone, not only threatening to the herd, but often to the one that pulls out. It is therefore difficult, but not impossible, and clearly essential, for some business leaders on some issues to participate positively in their formulation and adoption. Marcor-Wards started alone in its support for the CPA bill. For a long time we stayed alone. Now Polaroid, Zenith, Dreyfus Fund, Motorola, and Connecticut General Life are there. In fact, some 40 other companies are now publicly on record in support, and the number will continue to grow.

It's a sign that an increasing number of forward-looking companies are beginning to practice positive participation in the legislative arena. That is encouraging, but there is a kind of Dr. Jekyll and Mr. Hyde syndrome for business. On the one hand, there is extraordinary pragmatism, the ability to forcast change by early warning systems and to adapt rapidly to it to take advantage of it in the marketplace; on the other hand, there is hardening of the arteries and lack of adaptability in the legislative arena.

Businessmen must apply their extraordinary ability to count and to analyze to the legislative arena. Businessmen count extraordinarily well in business matters such as sales, inventory, and capital investment. But when you get to the legislative arena, and the U.S. Senate votes, 74 to 4, in favor of a preliminary bill for the Consumer Protection Agency, that 74 to 4 vote, with a similar vote on the House side, ought to say something significant to the business community other than just to keep saying "no." But we really are not able to count as well in the legislative arena as we do in the marketplace. We also do not always analyze our subject as carefully. We do not do our homework as thoroughly. We paint ourselves into corners of public all-out opposition too early, and thus lose our bargaining power.

We are making progress, but the question is whether that progress will be too little, too late. Public confidence in our institutions, including business, is sinking rapidly. We are all together on a Titantic, but it is a ship that still can make it through the storm if we shift our weight from negative opposition to positive participation in the legislative process. It does no good for any business leader to tell himself, or the passengers, that the ship has merely stopped to take on ice.

# Discussion

*Questions:* What are your comments on the intervention of the CPA into the informal proceedings of other government agencies? What is your response to the rumor that the acquisition of Marcor by Mobil is going to change the attitude of Marcor toward the Consumer Protection Act?

*Jones:* I had not heard about the rumor or report that, since Mobil acquired us, we have ceased to support CPA. There isn't one word of truth to it. We have worked from the day we got into this thing, and that was two years ago, as hard as we could to get a decent CPA bill, because the bill that passed 74 to 4 was lousy, wide open, with inadequate safeguards for the other government agencies, inadequate safeguards for business, inadequate notice provisions, badly drafted. Even the sponsors admitted it had some serious problems. It's one the reasons we got into the act. But we have worked hard for the passage of this bill and for getting safeguards not for special interest safeguards to kill it, or to emasculate it to the point where it won't accomplish its basic purpose, but safeguards that will make it work, in terms of administrative agency law and in terms of decent safeguards for business and any individual citizen. Up until one week before this last vote, not only did the chief executive officer of Montgomery Ward, Ed Donnell, also the president of Marcor, send out a new letter to every one of the 100 Senators, urging them to support this and giving the reasons why, but our Washington office did practically nothing else for the last two weeks before that final filibuster vote (when someone was late by 30 seconds) but to try and get this thing through. We were, quite honestly, one of the few companies that still had effective communications and working relations with all the sponsoring Senators and their staffs on this issue. It is very interesting to note that, all during that time, we were constantly being asked by various members of the business community to see if some of the provisions in the bill couldn't be tightened further. There were several we drafted at the last minute and had accepted by the sponsoring Senators (and by some others too, like Senator Aiken, who had voted for filibuster until we worked out the "Aiken Amendment," and then he voted against the filibuster).

Right down to the very last minute, we were hard at work on this one, also for some further amendments the business community wanted.

The question of CPA intervention in the informal proceedings of other government agencies is an example of the "keep your powder dry" rule, which we believe all business should bear in mind as a general guide. This doesn't apply just to the CPA. It really applies to business, or any other group, working on any legislation.

After the CPA bill passed the Senate in a preliminary version 74 to 4, for six months we spent a lot of time going over it, line by line, and paragraph by paragraph, making suggestions to the committee staff for possible changes, a number of which were accepted—simply because they thought it improved the bill. The bill passed the Government Operations Committee, 15 to 5, and it still had some problems, and no support from anyone in the business community, including ourselves. Up to this point we had never even discussed with the staff the possibility of our publicly supporting this thing. We had no notion whether we would ever support it. We just knew it was likely to pass sooner or later, that it had been badly in need of improvement after the Senate approved it preliminarily 74 to 4, that it had been significantly tightened during the six months, and that it still had several problems.

There were two essential changes needed: One concerned the informal proceedings-equal opportunity problem, the other, information gathering safeguards. If the bill when passed into law contained the phrase "equal opportunity" for the CPA in all informal proceedings of regulatory agencies, the courts would correctly interpret the phrase to mean the CPA must be given equal time and permitted to be present at all informal proceedings, including, for example, exploratory meetings between agency staff and a corporation which that corporation might have initiated to determine whether it had a problem and how best to solve it. Such a provision would discourage companies and staff from using informal proceedings and would make the government's task much harder. Instead, the bill ought to give the CPA a full (not equal) opportunity to present their views, meaning they don't have to be there simultaneously.

We took that and another amendment regarding additional safeguards on information gathering to the sponsors and they accepted all of the first and most of the second. But although the lawyer who had helped prepare the amendments for us was working to get an acceptable bill, some of his clients were working with the Senators to see if they couldn't kill it. They found they had painted themselves into a corner. They had become so involved with the Senators and their staffs in trying to kill the bill that they felt they could not now reverse field and publicly support it, even though the attorney had gotten it to the point that made it acceptable. That's what happens sometimes when you don't keep your powder dry, or when you play both sides of the fence without preserving your right to change your position.

*Question:* What kind of pressure do you expect to encounter as a result of your support of this legislation?

*Jones:* The only form of arm twisting you get a lot of would be better characterized as perfectly fair arguments and efforts to persuade us that we're wrong on the merits: a suggestion that you're out of your mind to support the creation of any new government agency, that we should all stick together, that the judicial review provision is wrong, or some other provision is harmful or bad law. But of all the legislative proposals you can actively support with less fear that they are going to bring about the end of private enterprise and with reasonable hope they will strengthen and help private enterprise and public confidence it it, these are the ones. Consumer views can be heard. There are no regulatory powers at all. It's got enough power to get information, so if someone is doing something seriously wrong, he is going to get in trouble, and that's just fine, since at least 95 percent of business at least 95 percent of the time isn't doing anything wrong, but still gets tarnished by those that do. This is not the super-agency monster that is going to destroy private enterprise, as a lot of representatives of business have been saying it is. There's now only one way we've got to prove that we're right and they're wrong. That is to have this thing created, and show that it isn't the monster some people have said it is.

*Question:* Is much of the hysteria over the Consumer Protection Agency Bill created by the Washington-based trade associations, and the representatives whose hidden agenda was really their own preservation rather than that of the company?

*Jones:* There may be some truth in that, although that thesis can be over-done like all others. Once you commit to oppose something, and these trade associations in perfectly good faith are committed, there are lots of issues they can do battle on, lots of work to be done, and one technique too often used by many of us to oppose something is to exaggerate its evil consequences. But I should add that when the CPA bill first passed the Senate 74 to 4 in preliminary form in 1971, it really did have very few safeguards, and it was something of a monster bill. It could have fouled up the other government agencies as well as the private citizen.

All we were really urging business to do more of was to get down there on the field of battle and grapple with the real issues of the bill, try to make it better. You do not have to make any advance commitments that you are going to support it, but get down on the battlefield and work in good faith, bargain in good faith, and negotiate in good faith. Then if you do get where it's 85 percent of what you think you can comfortably live with, on occasion, come out and indicate your willingness to consider supporting it. In the process of being amenable to the possibility of supporting it, you will likely accomplish still further changes.

But, rather than do that, some of the Washington reps declared early that this was a monster, and they were going to do all they could to kill it before it killed them, and unconditional surrender and battle to the death became the watch cry. So far they've been successful, against all of the forecasts, including Mike Mansfield's, who thought we were going to get that thing through two years ago.

We want all the companies we can get to join up in supporting CPA, and we've been working hard, with some success, to accomplish this. For one company to be in favor of the CPA and all the rest of the business community to be opposing it, still allows everyone who is antibusiness to say the business community is still negative, still protecting only the status quo.

*Question:* Did you say your initial purpose in going out and, in fact, supporting the bill was that it was a bad bill, but it was inevitable that it would pass and, therefore, it was necessary to get the best possible bill.

*Jones:* That's not what I said. All of the correspondence on this, between our chief executive officer and the sponsoring Senators, are all public documents; most are in the *Congressional Record.* After the bill passed 74 to 4, we said it looked like a good idea in principle, that its time had come, but the way it passed in preliminary form, there were four major areas we were very troubled by. We set down the four areas we thought were the worst problems, all four of which over the three-year period have been fully corrected.

There are letters in the Congressional Record from our top business people saying that the consumer feels he doesn't have a voice; that big business, big labor, and big government all make everyone feel some of the time that individuals are in a sea of impersonal forces they cannot possibly control. If you don't give consumer views a day in court, people are just going to feel more frustrated and angry and helpless than ever. All of us like to have a day in court, a chance to argue our case.

*Comment:* You've been emphasizing that corporations feel threatened. One of the things that surprises me is that big corporations are threatened by revolutions that don't seem very threatening to me, such as what kind of hiring process you have.

*Jones:* No one is threatened by any revolutionary change if he responds positively to it with confidence that, properly handled, it can be a step forward for everyone—political campaign disclosure, or Council on Economic Priorities' EEOC disclosure program. A lot of companies in the beginning were worried about getting into that in detail in their reports to the council, since the law is constantly changing, the standards are constantly evolving. I was one of many who helped write and pass the Civil Rights Act for 1964, including Title 7. I believe in it, but it's got some very general standards, and the EEOC and the Labor Department and the courts are constantly defining what some of those broad terms mean. Many times when a federal court gets into the act, it ups the standards compared to what the EEOC said. The concern of some of these companies in that area is that if we put up front what we are doing in this area, it's almost never enough. No comapny has yet gotten as far along as they will be three years or five years from now, even those that have launched very broad affirmative action programs. You really don't want everyone beating on your door if you are already working directly with EEOC or the Labor Department in an affirmative action program. You'll find there are, at times, reasonable reasons why people don't want to do this. Now frankly on that one, it's been done anyway. Virtually all the major companies the council asked have come out and have done it.

All major companies are already working to comply with federal laws and regulations, and many are also working with various federal government agencies with responsibilities in the EEO area. All the major companies, nearly all in *Fortune* 500, have a sense of responsibility in this, know what the law is, also

know what the consequences are if you don't move forward, and all the companies I know, including our own, are killing themselves to comply. We've already designed an affirmative action program and we are working like dogs to
find capable people, minorities, and women, to fill these positions. One of the
things I was concerned about in giving information to a private investigative
group was that someone might make an irresponsible response to a company
voluntarily providing its EEO data. If the private groups start beating on us on
top of the government agencies, when we're doing all we can, I am personally
going to get into the act. Something like that could kill the willingness of business to cooperate. This relates to all the other private consumer organizations,
too. How many do we have to deal with on any one issue? Twelve? A high
sense of balance, moderation, and cooperation is required from all sides if this is
going to truly serve the public interest.

*Question:* Who will get companies to pay attention to the figures they are
fishing out every year and sending to the government, that no one looks at?

*Jones:* That part we have absolutely no objection to. That's really the reason we were one of those that agreed to give the figures. But if someone either
finds an error, or thinks we are more deficient than most any other company,
and goes to the government with it, I would suggest giving notice to the corporation at the same time. If you found something, and you went to the company
first, then you could go to the government agency if the company didn't satisfy
you that they acted reasonably in trying to move ahead.

*Question;* When an outside group offers a shareholder resolution for the
purpose of getting information, do you think it is reasonable for management to
reject it for no reason other than that (it doesn't) want to give it?

*Jones:* No. We had a request last year that we thought was reasonable.
Someone wanted us to publish in a proxy statement full information on the
background of each of our directors. We had not been doing so, frankly, because three years earlier we had decided to try and put in more information
about each one of our directors. But we got into a hassle with one of the young
technicians at SEC. He wanted more, and more, and more. It took so long that
our management got frustrated and decided to forget it since it wasn't required.
So you are not going to get a blanket "no" without any reasons from us or from
most other companies. Whether we agree or disagree, you'll normally get a rea-
soned response.

It's terribly important to remember where all the trouble for the business
community comes from. Nine times out of ten it comes not only from Democrats, but from liberal Democrats, because they are the ones who want to reform
the system. The business community frequently doesn't talk to the liberal
Democratic Senators. It won't go near them, because it is scared to death, or
mad, or both. But it isn't that way in the Senate, and that attitude isn't the way
to protect your legitimate interests in the Senate. Business ought periodically to
support something that's reasonable, even if it isn't perfect, and also it ought to

spend more time advocating its views and hard facts to liberal Democratic
Senators.

About a year after we came out with our support for the Consumer Protection Agency bill, Senator Proxmire, without any warning to us, came out with
an amendment to the federal law on consumer credit. His proposal would have
required, by federal law, that every retailer use adjusted balance, which would
have cost most retailers, who provide consumer credit, 8 percent of their credit
revenues. We had just about a week to say, "No, this is wrong." He lost by one
vote, and next year we knew he was going to come back. We had come out for
the Consumer Protection Bill the year before. Three of us talked to about 60
Senators with hard, well-documented facts on the Proxmire proposal and the
harmful, unfair impact it would have on the public and especially the poor. But
we concentrated on liberal Democratic Senators, who had almost never voted for
business. It is like an advocacy proceeding in a court room. If you have done
your homework, and particularly if you've got a little credibility because you
supported the Consumer Protection Bill or some other proconsumer proposal,
they'll let you in the door, and listen receptively. And their final decision at
times will be in favor of part or all of your position—if you have the hard facts
and the merits of the argument on your side, and especially if you haven't always opposed to everything liberal Democrats favor. The vote this time, instead
of being 38 to 38, was 56 to 33 against Proxmire. All you've got to do is get in
there, and talk to them, and they'll listen every time. On more than one occasion, if you've got the facts and the merits of the argument on your side, they'll
vote your way, even if it's unpopular with some of their constituents. If you
have occasionally supported a consumer proposal, that won't hurt your case one
bit.

# 8

## Some Aspects of Information for Consumers
### William Haddon, Jr.

The supplying of product information is an ancient practice including in its origins utility in marketplace identification, the pride of the makers of objects, and the needs of governments. Although there are much earlier examples of each, it is useful to consider the history of the hallmarking of silver and gold objects made in England, since it illustrates both that our century is by no means the first in which such product information matters have been addressed, and that three-way relationships among makers (and suppliers), purchasers, and governments are an old story.

By act of 1300 all plate made in England was required to carry the punch of the Leopard's Head. It also ordained:

> .... no goldsmith of England, nor none otherwhere within the King's dominion . . . shall from henceforth make or cause to be made any manner of vessel, jewel or any other thing of gold or silver, except it be of good and true allay [sic], that is to say, gold of a certain touch, and silver of the esterling allay or of better, at the pleasure of him to whom the work belongeth; . . . and that no manner of vessel of silver depart out of the hands of the workers until it be assayed by the gardiens of the Craft, and further that it be marked with a leapard's head; and that they work no worse gold than of the touch of Paris; and that the wardens of the Craft shall go from shop to shop among the goldsmiths to essay if their gold be of [that] touch. . . . And that all the good towns of England, where any goldsmith be dwelling, shall be ordered according to this statute as they of London be; and that one shall come from every good town for all the residue that be dwelling in the same unto London for to be ascertained of their touch.[1]

Export restrictions followed in 1335 and 1381, and in 1363 the "maker's mark" was required.

> Every master goldsmith[a] "should have a mark by himself, which mark shall be known by them assigmed by the King to survey their work and allay; . . . and that after the assay made the surveyor should set the King's mark (Leopard's Head) upon it, and then the goldsmith his mark for which he should answer." Plate made between 1364 and 1458 should thus bear two punched marks. The Act also restricted the price of silver.[2]

---

It gives me great pleasure to acknowledge the able and creative assistance of my son Jonathan W. Haddon in our initial scrutiny of diverse products in exploring the information given with them, and later, in formulating a general approach.

[a]The term included workers in both gold and silver.

As one commentator has written,

. . . the fourteenth century was thus remarkable for continual efforts by the legislature and the goldsmiths themselves to keep gold and silver within the kingdom, to standardize the quality of plate throughout the county so that the public might be protected from fraud and the trade from lack of public confidence, and to allocate the responsibility for such frauds directly to the guilty maker or to the conniving or inefficient official. England, however, was not alone, nor even the leader, in such reforms, which were based on the regulations evolved in France, particularly in Paris and at Montpellier.[3]

The years that followed saw many elaborations on the same theme, for example: controls on what objects could be plated, and how (1403); mandatory purchase of silver brought to the Master of the Mint, use of experts to adjudicate its value, and delegation of authority to provincial "assay towns" (1423); the introduction of a third compulsory stamp, the annual "date letter" (1477); the indictment of two goldsmiths "for making divers parcels of counterfeit plate debased" (1597). In summarizing the reasons for this system and the interests of the public, makers and sellers, and government, Gerald Taylor has written,

Thus after nearly three hundred years of parliamentary legislation and regulations devised by officers of the Goldsmiths' Company, there was established an enforceable system of controls whereby the purchaser of plate could with confidence buy gold and silver wares of guaranteed quality, or, if he had cause for complaint, seek redress at law against the officers of the Goldsmiths' Company or the goldsmith, or both. The statutes were generally designed to protect public interests in the widest sense, giving the individual purchaser the protection he needed against easily practised frauds through the common law, ensuring that the economic position of the country was not upset through lack of currency, preventing the provincial goldsmiths from being ruined by their more powerfully organized London rivals and ensuring that the elected officers of the London and provincial companies did their duties honestly and impartially. The London goldsmiths themselves devised an effective administrative machinery to execute the will of Parliament without placing unduly heavy burdens on any member of their mystery. Thereafter, the system was only adjusted in detail and not in principle.[4]

Although the history of hallmarking provides especially clear-cut illustration of principal reasons for providing product information and some of the patterns as to how the several interests have been accommodated, examples involving other products (and more recently services) are legion. Moreover, since the needs for such information extend across the breadth and complexity of commerce and are unique only at the level of very specific characteristics of some products (for example, the percentage of silver in an alloy), it is hardly surprising that product information may logically be grouped into several fairly discrete categories.

In exploring this, I decided to define the groupings of product information I found on the basis of questions to which such information responds. Table 8–1 gives the five groups that resulted. In tables 8–2 through 8–6 I have elaborated on each of these in turn and illustrated with actual examples, running from an endorsement from an old (probably nineteenth century) patent medicine circular to a federally mandated new vehicle certification.

For brevity, I have principally addressed *product* information rather than that about *services*. But a closely analogous approach using the same general groupings and many, if not most, of the secondary ones serves equally well, although more attention is often needed in the case of services to the "conditions," the "fine print" as it were. It is also noteworthy that individual product information terms often incorporate more than one item of information. Thus, "pasteurized" indicates both a process and a quality.

I have also not addressed the complex, interrelated area of how such information can best be presented, to insure minimum error in transmission and maximum breadth and depth of receipt and comprehension among its targets. That such problems are highly diverse and important is well known, for example, to businessmen seeking product recognition and market penetration; to government regulators seeking to recall products unnecessarily posing threats to health; and to members of the public confronted with the almost limitless problems of satisfactory marketplace choice and subsequent product use. Specific examples include errors in the reading of labels on pharmaceuticals and the fact that the petroleum distillates a manufacturer of a product such as a bug spray from his standpoint labels as "inert" may be medically highly poisonous if they enter the body.[b]

I have also not dealt with the equally diverse legal aspects of product information. However, it seems to me that for these and many other ancillary aspects of consumer information it will be frequently useful to have a basic framework against which to consider specific issues, an introductory tool for thinking about, for sorting facts and problems. As such, the outline I have presented should be viewed as one way of approaching this area. As with any other tool, it should be employed, modified, or supplanted as appropriate to the needs and problems addressed. It does demonstrate, however, that it is possible, and very useful, to generalize as to the varieties of information that are or may be supplied on or about products and services.

## Notes

1. Gerald Taylor, *Silver,* 2nd ed. (Baltimore: Penguin Books, 1963), 302 pp.
2. Ibid.
3. Ibid.
4. Ibid.

---

[b]I am indebted to Ms. Susan P. Baker, assistant professor, The Johns Hopkins University, School of Hygiene and Public Health, for calling my attention to the problem of so called "inert ingredients."

**Table 8-1. Five Categories of Consumer Information Defined by Questions to Which Such Information Responds**

1. Who produced it?
2. What was produced?
3. What are the conditions of sale?
4. What are the instructions for use?
5. What are the benefits of use?

**Table 8-2. Kinds of Information Provided in the "Who Produced it?" Category of Consumer Information**

| People and Organizations Involved | Identities | | Locations |
| --- | --- | --- | --- |
| | Actual | Representations | |
| Makers, processors, middlemen, distributors, shippers, agents, sellers | Paul Revere | PR (silversmith maker's mark) | Boston, Massachusetts |
| | The Drackett Products Company | Drano (a brand name) | Cincinnati, Ohio |
| | Safeway Stores, Incorporated | Logo and trademark (combined in this case) (not here reproduced) | Oakland, California |

**Table 8-3. Kinds of Information Provided in the "What Was Produced?" Category of Consumer Information**

| Items | Examples |
| --- | --- |
| A. How and of what produced? | |
| 1. Ingredients, contents | |
| a. Plant | Cayenne pepper. Grown originally in the Cayenne district of Africa, now in California |
| b. Animal | Fancy albacore white tuna |
| c. Inanimate mixture | Sea salt |
| d. Molecular | Ascorbic acid, niacin, sorbitol, BHT, sodium phosphate, thiamin |
| 2. Components | |
| a. Mechanical | Automatic transmission |
| b. Electronic | All solid state |
| 3. Processes and transformations | Pasteurized, frozen, sterilized, vacuum packed, freeze dried, distilled |
| B What is the result? | |
| 1. Final product | Milk, lager beer, Waiting at the Church (a piano roll), shrub and hedge trimmer |
| 2. Maker, seller's designation | 6½% preferred, hip huggers |

|   |   |
|---|---|
| 3. Weight | Net wt. 12 oz., 737 grams |
| 4. Volume | 4½ fl. oz., 1.5 liters |
| 5. Age | 8 years old (scotch) |
| 6. When produced | September 17, 1974 |
| 7. Size | Size 12, large, 75 watts |
| 8. Grade | Grade A, U.S.D.A. prime, fancy |
| 9. Percent composition | Sodium hydroxide 54.20%, 2% fat, 5% acidity, 100% orange juice |

**Table 8-4. Kinds of Information Provided in the "What Are the Conditions of Sale?" Category of Consumer Information**

| *Items* | *Examples* |
|---|---|
| Number produced | An edition of five hundred |
| Cost | 2 for 99¢, $2350, 50¢ and 2 Cheerios Play-Doh proof-of-purchase seals |
| Conditions | |
| Warranties and reservations | Manufacturer's only obligation shall be to replace such quantity of the product proved to be defective. User shall determine the suitability of the product for his intended use, and assume all risks and liability therewith. All rights of the manufacturer and of the owner of the recorded work reserved. Unauthorized public performance, broadcasting and copying of this record prohibited. |
| | Copyright 1964 by the Association for the Aid of Crippled Children |
| Places where obtainable | At authorized dealers Coast to Coast |
| Times when obtainable | Weekdays 9-5, Saturdays 9-1 |

**Table 8-5. Kinds of Information Provided in the "What Are the Instructions for Use?" Category of Consumer Information**

| *Items* | *Examples* |
|---|---|
| Period usable | Develop before May 1976 |
| Who or for what intended | For "Instamatic" cameras |
| Purpose | To remove household odors For headache and minor arthritic pain |
| How begin | Open on dotted line Sign on dotted line |
| How prepare | Mix with three cans cold water. .Stir or shake briskly |

**Table 8-5. Continued**

| Items | Examples |
|---|---|
| Condition signals | Operable pressure indicators on fire extinguishers |
| | Color indicators of sterility in suture and surgical instrument packs |
| How use | Take one every four hours |
| | Connect to TV antenna |
| Warnings | DANGER. Contains sodium hydroxide (caustic soda-lye). Corrosive: causes severe eye and skin damage. Keep Drano and solutions of Drano away from eyes, skin and clothing; don't get it on you. *Always keep out of reach of children.* Harmful or fatal if swallowed |
| | CAUTION—TO PREVENT ELECTRIC SHOCK, DO NOT REMOVE COVER. NO USER SERVICEABLE PARTS INSIDE. REFER SERVICING TO QUALIFIED SERVICE PERSONNEL. |
| | CAUTION: DO NOT USE IN RAIN. REPLACE DAMAGED CORD IMMEDIATELY. |
| Emergency measures | ANTIDOTES EYES—immediately flood with water for at least 20 minutes. Follow with 5% Boric Acid solution . . . . |

**Table 8-6. Kinds of Information Provided in the "What Are the Benefits of Use?" Category of Consumer Information**

| Items | Examples |
|---|---|
| Claims, running from the objectively provable to the unsupportable | |
|   1. Certifications | This vehicle conforms to all applicable Federal Motor Vehicle Safety Standards in effect on the date of manufacture shown abo◖ |
|   2. Health | Destroys most disease germs |
| | Provides 30% of U.S. Recommended Daily Allowance (U.S.R.D.A |
| | 'Ouchless' Telfa won't stick to healing skin |
|   3. Financial | For loss of hand or foot, $75,000 |
|   4. Personality | Why be a wallflower. Become the life of the party! |
|   5. Appearance | Makes you look years younger |
|   6. Elimination of nuisances | Prevents damp basements |
| Premiums | Kenner offers you up to $22 in Toy Savings! Cash refund book inside |
| Endorsements | After using salves and Blood Purifiers for twenty years, I most cheerfully testify that nothing has ever afforded such ease and freedom from pain and itching as PIKE'S CENTENNIAL SALT RHEUM SALVE. I take real pleasure in showing my fingers, and telling friends how good they feel |
| | GREENFIELD T. SAWYER, 110 State St., Boston |

The business community has been the principal (albeit not the sole) target of the
activities and demands of consumerism. Business's reactions have varied—accepting, being cautious, and rejecting—in response to consumerism's efforts to increase
the rights and powers of buyers in relation to sellers. Whatever one's personal
perspective on consumerism, however, the business community obviously looks
upon consumerism with growing interest and concern. Clearly, businessmen's
opinions on consumerism—its past, present, and future—are pertinent.

This chapter reports on the results on a comprehensive survey of executives' attitudes toward consumerism. Conducted with the joint sponsorship of
the *Harvard Business Review* and the Marketing Science Institute, the study ex-
amines and interprets the opinions of over 3,400 businessmen. Among the issues treated in terms of businessmen's perceptions are the causes and growth of
consumerism, its impact on marketing and other business practices, present and
prospective business reactions to it, and its regulatory ramifications.

This is the first wide-scale study of the attitudes held in the business community on these issues. This report offers a summary of the major findings,
and concentrates on those findings of broadest interest. A more extensive review and discussion of the study results, prepared with my collaborator, Steven
Diamond, has been published in the *Harvard Business Review*,[1] from which por-
tions of this presentation are adapted.

## Methodology and Respondents

The *Harvard Business Review* (*HBR*) article includes a careful description of
the methodology. Basically the study consisted of two, matched eight-page
questionnaires, composed of agree-disagree statements, and some ranking and
check-off questions. The questionnaires were mailed to split halves of a random-
ly selected cross-section of *HBR* subscribers, with one follow-up mailing. Many
of the specific questions were worded in both a pro-business and antibusiness
form in order to probe both sides of a given issue fairly. Each form of the questionnaire was balanced between statements favorable and unfavorable to business.

The respondents, representing about 28 percent of those to whom the questionnaire was mailed, come from a wide variety of industries, company sizes,
functional areas, and levels of management. Naturally, a large proportion—about
half—are in industries and companies where marketing is considered particularly

important. The respondents include many with direct experience with consumerism and many who have been relatively unaffected by it. Obviously, a traditional caveat pertains: While past surveys of similar respondents (i.e., *HBR* subscribers) suggest that attitudes of nonrespondents differ little (other than in terms of indifference) from those of respondents, we have no definitive evidence on this in the present study.

**Major Findings**

Let me review the principal findings regarding executives' views on consumerism, again noting in so doing that these are *attitudes*, not necessarily substantive realities, regarding consumerism.

Overall, as stated in the *HBR* article, there is: . . . broad recognition and acceptance of consumerism by managers as a permanent part of the business landscape. Although some of this acceptance is grudging, a strong majority of executives consider consumerism a positive force in the marketplace. Moreover, by far the most dominant management view of consumerism is that it represents an opportunity for marketers rather than a threat to them.[2]

     More specifically:

*Here to Stay*

Businessmen strongly agree (84%) that consumerism is "here to stay." Why? When asked to appraise the relative importance of a variety of claimed economic, social, and business-specific causes of consumerism's growth, responding executives rank consumer concern over rising prices as the leading cause of consumerism's growth. A cluster of product performance and quality problems—both real and as perceived by consumers—are the next most frequently mentioned causes; these include consumers feeling a growing gap between product performance and marketing claims. In terms of specific business and marketing practices that cause consumer dissatisfaction, product problems are considered the most important. Defective products, hazardous or unsafe products, and defective repair work or service are the three most frequently mentioned causes of consumer problems and dissatisfactions.

*Consumer Disillusion*

Respondents see a dip in consumer confidence in both the marketplace and marketers. Most (76%) take the view that "consumer disillusionment today is higher than in the past."

*Buyer Beware Eroding*

Executives see the pendulum shifting from "buyer beware" to "seller beware." Using a 7-point scale to characterize the marketplace balance between the two, their assessments are:

Today:     3.2 (about the midpoint)

1980:      4.9 (shift toward seller beware)

Ideal:     4.6 (more strongly toward seller beware than now, but not so
           far as the predicted 1980 position)

*Marketing and Consumer Power*

Consumerists and marketers seem to have different opinions about how the marketplace works. For example, consumerists typically claim that consumers often do not make the right buying decisions, and that marketers' efforts often confuse (or even mislead) consumers. Not unexpectedly, executives take issue with such contentions. By a 2 to 1 margin, executives see consumers as "generally making the right buying decisions in terms of their own wants and values," and by a 3 to 2 margin as "making highly self-satisfying product choices, even under complex circumstances." Executives also express confidence in consumer power. By almost a 4 to 1 margin, executive believe "consumers can most effectively voice their discontent with products by not buying them."

*Advertising Issues*

Advertising, perhaps because of its high visibility, has been the target of considerable consumerist criticism. Responding executives express concern over misleading advertising and over marketing's general tendency to promise too much. Executives also offer surprisingly strong support for a number of propositions that would make advertising more factual and informative, related to the majority's skepticism over advertising's truthfulness.

Not surprisingly, virtually all executives (96%) agree that "advertisers should be forced to substantiate their claims," since advertisers are already required to do so. But almost as many (87%) agree that "advertising should include information for 'logical' buying decisions, whether or not consumers choose to use it." That "advertising should be limited to factual and emotional information," draws support from about half (51%) of the respondents. Further, there is executive support for the general notion that "markets should make a sincere effort to point out the failings and limitations of their products as well as their strengths" (62% agree). Thus, there is surprising sympathy for some of the more restrictive ideas about advertising that have been put forward by consumerists, and a strong majority vote (76%–19%) that "consumerism will lead to major modifications in advertising content."

### Causing and Remedying Consumer Problems

The triangle of government, business, and consumers is involved in any assessment of the causes and remedies of consumer problems. Executives assign to business the dominant (about 50%) share for both cause and remedy. In terms of specific areas of remedial responsibility, executives consider government to have the principal role in protecting consumers from clear-cut abuses in the marketplace, although business is the overwhelming choice to provide adequate information to assist consumers in making purchase decisions. However, consumers are seen as carrying the primary burden in setting their own appropriate buying priorities. With regard to protecting consumers from their own buying mistakes, executives see mixed responsibilities, with consumers carrying primary responsibility, but with government and business (respectively) playing a role. Executives seem overall to favor traditional reliance on business self-regulation to remedy consumer travails, but with a moderate role for government and with definite responsibilities for consumers.

### Corporate Responses

Executives evince a remarkable uniformity of opinion as to the most constructive consumer-oriented programs companies should undertake. In response to a question seeking the most constructive consumer programs, considering their own industries as the frame of reference, executives far and away considered *upgrading product quality and performance standards* as first choice. (Detailed responses for the ten most frequently mentioned programs, by industry, appear in the *HBR* article.)

### Progress?

Executives also offered their perceptions on the rate of progress on consumer issues, comparing their impressions of today's conditions with those of ten years ago and with those they expect to exist ten years from now. Among the five key consumer-related dimensions evaluated, company sensitivity to consumer complaints is considered the area of most progress in the past ten years. The quality of repair and maintenance services is rated as having the least relative progress in the past decade.

*Differing Opinions*

Naturally, not all executives see these issues in the same way. The *HBR* article offers some specific variations, many of which relate to the extent to which consumerism has had an impact on the responding executives' firms.

## Overview

The study permits some overall assessment of businessmen's appraisal of consumerism, not only from the specific findings reviewed above (and in the article-length report) but also from some questions directly addressed to their broad perspectives on consumerism.

Businessmen strongly believe that "companies can capitalize on consumerism as a competitive marketing tool." Some 89 percent agree with this claim. Further, they see consumerism as "a positive force in the marketplace" (71%), not a negative one (13%). Executives seem to be saying that consumerism is good for the consumer and good for business.

In essence, it appears—at least in terms of this study—that consumerism is no longer considered anathema by management. It is seen as a positive force— one that has brought about a genuine change in business practices, one that can both benefit business and improve the consumer's lot.

## Notes

1. Stephen A. Greyser and Steven L. Diamond, "Business is Adapting to Consumerism," *Harvard Business Review,* September–October 1974.

2. Ibid.

# 10 Where Is Consumerism Going?
*Mark Green*

I have always pondered the origin of the term "consumerism." In a more para-noid moment it seemed that a malignant critic had tried to phonetically com-pare it to communism. Stick as "ism" at the end of a word and it sounds some-what threatening. In that, they surely have failed, just as similar critics did with the Children's Crusade and muckrakers, both of which titles were originally intended as derisive but instead became a kind of badge of honor and identifi-cation.

Even those who are not proud of the phrase consumerism cannot doubt its popularity, at least as measured by polls, which is one guage of popularity. Ac-cording to polls conducted by Louis Harris Associates,[1] 81 to 10 percent of res-pondents agree that if a firm's advertising is false or misleading, it should be pro-hibited from advertising for a certain period; 75 to 14 percent agree that major companies should set strict standards of quality to be enforced by government in-spection; 51 to 29 percent felt that in lawsuits over faulty or defective products, the officers of major companies should be held personally responsible.

The interesting thing about consumerism is not that it is popular, but that it has not always converted itself into real policy. Part of the problem is that there are many people in the academic community, and hence in government, who are still not sympathetic to its basic premise, which is that while the free market system can be an efficient innovator and push down prices, it is not omniscient. The most outspoken opponent of the point of view that the less government, the better in the consumer area is Professor Milton Friedman of the University of Chicago's department of economics. He was the subject of a fas-cinating profile in *Playboy* a couple of years ago where he said that you do not need environmental protection laws because if Gary, Indiana has too much pollu-tion because of a steel plant, then workers will not stay and work; and Gary will then have an incentive to reduce its pollution. If you have a consumer problem, he added, you go to court and you sue; or if the product is bad the consumer eventually will not buy it.[2] Of course, there are still workers in Gary, Indiana, al-though it is an environmentally dangerous area. Why? Because there are labor shortages and there is no easy mobility. Also, you cannot just sue. The costs of going to court, and lawyers fees are prohibitive for most Americans. Sometimes consumers learn about the danger of a product by taking it and being harmed. A most lethal example of this occurred in 1937 when a drug misnamed Elixir Sulfanamide took 107 lives, and *then* people realized they should not buy it. That is a gross example, but others make the same point; education by ingestion and then illness is hardly the way a system should work. We can do far better.

Where is consumerism going? The consumerist movement has had some major successes, but it may not be going anywhere in terms of the big sweep of history. Other movements have, like lightning, lit up the night, and then it was dark again, a quick flourish before the eclipse. Do you remember Stokley Carmichael or even the SCLC? The women's movement today has had a lot of successes but it is unclear where it is going. The same is true for consumer rights and those who advocate them. It is not clear whether consumerism has a sufficient power base to continue its progression. As one way to organize an examination of whether it will continue to flourish or not, I would like to propose five axioms that, depending on their fulfillment, could in a large measure determine whether consumerism will be a flash in the pan or a permanent institution in our country.

The first axiom is that consumerism is broad not narrow. Reporters, for instance, should not talk about small retail bilking: toasters that break shortly after purchase, warranties that do not warrant, or deliver. These can be serious problems, to be sure, but there is often such a focus on the buying experience, which is the one that we see and get involved in, that we can dissipate our efforts and end up tinkering with, but not reforming, the real problems.

Take hot dogs—the frankfurter represents a lot of things. What is its price? That we can see when we buy it. What does it look like? Without food coloring it would be brown, not red; but what does that mean in terms of what we take into our bodies? What about the nitrites in it? Who produces the hotdogs? How many firms produce hot dogs? Are they so few that, although we do not "see" it when we look at the label, the price inevitably is going to be higher? Because when few firms produce a product you do not have price competition, but rather parallel pricing, which characterizes oligopolies. Who owns the company that produces hot dogs? Is it a conglomerate? Then it is hard to figure out the profits and losses a conglomerate's division that produces hot dogs, but that means that someone can not know if there is monopoly pricing. You do not know if it is a failing company—and as a result investors cannot make decisions on whether to invest in that firm as wisely as they should. Or, for example, when you buy the product, is it so packaged that you can not actually see it?

There are a whole range of things that you should think about in order to perceive the process that produced the product. My emphasis here is to look at the process as well as the product. It is the process that determines the cost of the product as well as its quality.

We are now talking about the structure and organization and concentration of American industry. Who makes the decisions in corporations that affect the products we buy? The fact that there are three and a "half" American auto firms producing 97 percent of our domestic auto production means something in terms of prices we pay. It means something in terms of the quality of automobiles we purchase. Look at the oil industry. There are many more oil firms

than auto firms, but we have to ask: how are they structured? From explora-
tion to gas station they are what is called "vertically integrated"; there are far
fewer in the local areas, which is where competition exists or not, than there are
nationally—and that affects both the price we pay and the energy crisis. In this
analysis I would recommend for us to be "big thinkers." There are places for
little thinkers, those that analyze cost studies, and for big thinkers, like Galbraith who recoil at specific examples. I would also recommend a pamphlet
Beverly Moore has published: *A Modest Proposal for the Reform of the Capitalist System.*[3] Each represents a certain school of thought: Galbraith's is a
form of nationalization and socialism and Beverly Moore's is a form of tougher
capitalism and more competition.

A second axiom is that consumerism is politics. We do not think of politics when we think of consumerism. We think of products and bilks, which is
necessary but not sufficient. A political system by definition requires conflict.
I have never seen a total consensus on anything. Those who are interested in
consumerism have to reward their friends and punish their opponents. What
this means politically is that when a Senator Milton Young casts the deciding
vote not to create the Consumer Protection Agency, he has the right to do it and
his critics have a right to go into his home state and criticize it, lobby against it,
conduct press conferences, challenge him to debates. The voters of that state
have to know how that man voted because it is essential to reward and deter
votes on consumer issues.

Campaign finance reform—is that just something for Common Cause to talk
about or something for us to talk about? Historically big money has controlled
political judgments in this country. I am not talking about bribery; it is nothing
that simple, although occasionally it occurs. But you get your cues from, and
you answer the phone calls of, those people who have been kind enough to provide you with money to get into public office. A campaign finance bill recently
passed Congress, but *without* a provision for public financing of congressional
campaigns. I favor public financing because while it would cost us pennies apiece
out of the Treasury as taxpayers, it would save us hundreds and hundreds of
dollars apiece as consumers in the form of fewer preferential policies for business
—witness Richard Nixon's decision to raise milk price supports, after receiving a
large campaign contribution pledge, which cost American consumers $700,000,000
annually. That is politics and that is consumerism. You cannot divorce the two.

Consider the filibuster. Caricaturists draw Senators reading the weather report or the Bible, day after day, which is fatal to a democracy. If a chamber
cannot act democratically then I cannot see how it can represent a democracy.
Hence, Senator Allan and Senator Ervin almost single-handedly defeated the
Consumer Protection Agency bill. (It is now called the Agency for Consumer
Advocacy because certified public accountants got very upset at the shorthand
of CPA—a concession that really did not matter.) The rules have to be changed
to make them more fair, to represent the kind of popular interest in consumer

issues I have already described. Then popularity can get translated into policy
and law. Right now there is a blockage, because of the rules of the system and
because consumer groups have really not gone political.

It is essential to educate voters about the issues, but we are not doing it
successfully on the issue of consumerism. Name a recent election where the
consumer issue provided the margin of difference. In campaigns, saying we
should have a consumer protection agency bill gets zero news. If you attack
your opponent for taking a campaign contribution and then going against a
public finance bill, that makes news. There is a built-in bias in the system to
attack personalities rather than to discuss the merits of an issue.

A third axiom that will control the future of consumerism is that consumerism is not a point in time but a sequence. There is a whole process, a whole
sequence from the discussion of a law to its passage and to its implementation,
that will affect whether we have small or meaningful victories for consumerism
and whether it really changes the quality of peoples' lives. First comes the discussion of an issue. This involves largely the press, the media, the consumer
advocates, seminars. Then comes the congressional process. But even when a
law is passed, to what extent does it have real application to people's lives?
The expression for this in constitutional law is that constitutional law is what
the cop on the beat says it is. In other words, the Supreme Court can issue as
many grand rulings as it wants, but if local police chiefs ignore them, they have
no effect.

Let us look at the process beyond merely passing a bill. What is the appro-
priation level? It is in that latter stage when an agency can be created but effectively gutted because it simply lacks the manpower to do the job. What is the
quality of the staff and from where do they come? It seems apparent that the
Consumer Product Safety Commission recently, by fighting the White House
tooth and nail because the latter wanted the usual Civil Service type of appointment and the former wanted more independence, is significantly different from
the Federal Energy Administration, which is staffed at top levels by people from
the oil industry who are not unbiased. Consider the agencies operations and
programs. Who lobbies them? Is there any kind of lobbying registration requirement? We do not want to discourage anyone from lobbying an agency. The
first amendment demands that we have free access to the government, but that
does not prohibit the registration of lobbyists so that people can know who is
lobbying for whom and for how much and to what degree and on what issue.
More information is better than less information in a democracy where information is power. What are the ex parte rules of that agency? Can a few people
see commissioners without other people knowing about it? What happens in ex
parte meetings? Since fungus grows in unlit places, one is always suspicious,
especially in the light of recent scandals.

Does the agency provide for *in forma pauperis* proceedings, so that when
someone has a meritorious claim on its face, they can be provided with counsel

if they cannot afford to have counsel themselves? What are the regulations of the agency to implement its enabling act? A toy safety act was passed a few years ago and for months the Food and Drug administration refused to draft and implement regulations that would explain the law in order for it to be enforced. They finally adopted some regulations for the act around December 23 of the year after it was enacted, two days before the major holiday that most affects toy sales. The Department of Transportation for four years failed to draft required regulation on used cars and tires. After a law suit by Ralph Nader's litigation organization, the DOT, probably not entirely coincidentally, issued the regulations.

The "sequence of consumerism" also involves the quality of the appointees themselves to agencies. Here I would refer you to a book to be published in a year by Victor Kramer and his Institute for Public Interest Representation, which carefully studied the FTC and FCC appointees during the last 20 years in terms of their quality and political inspiration.[4]

Each level of this process from discussion of the issue to its actual enforcement can be critical. If you lose at any one point, you can lose the whole ball game. Those interested in consumerism must study the entire process and not focus on only one layer to the exclusion of others.

Fourth, I think that consumerism should focus on government and not on business. This judgment is grounded in my view—that it is easier to move government than business. If a power line is going over your land, how are you going to change the utilities' mind? At least the government has a premise of access to democracy. You throw the rascals out, although contradicting that last statement is the fact that something like 92 percent of all incumbents who run for office are reelected. But how exactly do you pressure a company to do something if it does not want to do it? There have been very few successful consumer boycotts in our history. Someone may say, "but there was a beef boycott last year and people did not buy beef." And a lot of people did not. Demand for beef went down; and then the price went *up.*

The corporate economy has changed, although peoples' perception of it has not. The reason I emphasize government more than business is that I have a skepticism about what is called corporate social responsibility. A Giant Food may hire an Esther Peterson, and both have good intentions to change the system of Giant to best serve the consumer. That is laudatory and it can be a model to other companies to do the same. But to depend on the voluntary virtue of business or any group that has a balance sheet, and must look at a balance sheet, is naive. If something should be done, it should be required, not permitted. Then the political system votes and it becomes public policy. If you think unit labeling and code dating are necessary, it should be required by law. Then business cannot complain that they are being disadvantaged if they are ahead of their competitor; it should be required of all equally. The cost should be borne by all equally. To an extent it will be passed on to consumers all equally, who will be paying for what will presumably be a better product.

Government itself can hurt consumers terribly, however. This theme—the government as a monopoly maker, raising prices because its regulations serve not consumers but producers—is an issue whose time has apparently come, at least for those of us who read the *Wall Street Journal* or the *New York Times.* There are many examples of this. A Nader group tried to compile the best scholarly studies of the costs of waste and overcharge in just the transportation and communication sectors, which they found totaled from 16 to 24 billion dollars annually—costs ultimately borne by consumers in the form of higher prices.

My fifth axiom is that consumerism depends on pressure groups pressuring government. It is built into the system. Our government is not always responsible, but it is reactive, which means it is not going to initiate something tomorrow because it has a good idea; it will or it will not take initiative depending on whether people pressure or do not pressure it to take certain action. Institutions that can apply pressure include of course the press. In Washington we have seen how the press can influence political events. They can also influence consumer events on Capital Hill and in local agencies and state agencies.

There are now several public-interest advocacy groups in Washington in the food and drug area such as the Center for Science in the Public Interest and the Health Research Group who create an environment that makes it impossible any longer for the agency simply to issue a casual anticonsumer ruling or fail to enforce the requirements of the 1962 Drug Amendments—as it did in the 1960s—which mandated that drugs must not only be safe but efficacious as well. It took FDA six years to get off the dime on that. In the past an FDA action might be criticized by drug firms or food firms. But now it may also be criticized by the public interest sector. Someone once said that a statesman is someone who feels equal pressure on all sides, which makes him stay upright. In order to keep an agency upright you have to lean on it from all sides.

In the past, too often issues were lost by default. Either agencies did not know enough to be more pro-consumer or they did not have any incentive to avoid public censure by a citizen's group dissatisfied with their various rulings. In 1969 the prime time access rule, which was then pending before the FCC, provoked 116 submissions by law firms or interested parties, broadcasters and networks to defeat the rule and only 4 submissions by groups or individuals who wanted more access to prime time. The natural result of that kind of inundation and one-sidedness is a commissioner who tends to think: I guess that is the better part of wisdom, given the *quantity* of the argument; forget the quality.

To avoid that tilt requires the creation of a core of public interest advocates —lawyers, scientists, engineers, doctors—who make it their business to monitor government. They provide a counterweight to business interests who are entitled to their point of view but who should not monopolize the process. However, you should not glorify public interest advocates, as some have. They have had some wins, and a lot of losses. In Washington, where I have studied their impact, there are 190 public interest lawyers operating on a budget of $13 million derived from foundations, attorneys' fees, Ralph Nader's lecture fees, and Public Citizen's and Common Cause's dues. But on the other side are 11,500 private attorneys in Washington representing business interests grossing an annual $307 million a year. The process is still one-sided, although not as much as before.

To conclude, I cannot go into the record here of what consumerism has been and done. But looking at its future, there are a number of needs, all of which go in the direction of making the assumptions of the consumer process real. Too often we dally in assumptions rather than work to change the reality of the corporate economy. We need more competition not less. We need tougher antitrust laws, bigger budgets, and penalties enforced against those who violate the laws. In the now 84-year history of antitrust laws, there have been four instances, just four, where business violators have actually gone to jail for antitrust crime. I am not excited to see people go to jail by the way, but if you sit down in a room and price fix, it is a *per se* offense; if the result is that millions of dollars go from consumers to producers, that is a criminal offense, just as damaging as stealing someone's money in the street—although it is not so perceived.

Corporations have been largely free from responsibility to the government that creates them. Witness state chartering agencies, which are often just mail drops, often a couple of people in a small room trying to monitor 50,000 firms that charter in their state. They are charades. The largest firms in our country engage in national business and they should be nationally chartered. This does not mean to take them over; it simply means they should be responsible to an institution of commensurate power. ITT is more powerful than Delaware. It could *buy* Delaware! We need the federal chartering of our largest corporations.

There also has to be more corporate disclosure, so that consumers, investors, government regulators, and members of Congress can know what is going on. Too often we are dependent on what we know about industry from the industry members themselves who have an interest in not being candid about what they disclose, as the Federal Power Commission has found out recently in scandal-sized headlines in Washington involving the faulty reporting of gas reserves.

All these issues are controversial. Ideas will succeed or fail in a clash in the turmoil of the marketplace of ideas. We cannot shirk that debate or that conflict; we cannot discuss these issues solely on the basis of Marquis de Queensbury rules. It is more clamorous than that. Happily it is not as it would be after a soccer match in Brazil or a coup in Chile; we will all survive for the next battle. But we cannot ignore the contest and the context of consumer affairs. Because ultimately for all of us, whatever we think, it is not only how you play the game, but if we really care about consumers, it is also whether you win or lose.

## Notes

1. See Green, "Appropriateness and Responsiveness: Can the Government

Protect the Consumer," *Journal of Economic Issues* VIII (June, 1974):309-328 (notes).

2.  "Interview with Milton Friedman," *Playboy* (March, 1973): 51 et. seq.

3.  Material can be obtained by writing to Beverly C. Moore, Jr., 4914 Belt Road, NW., Washington, D.C.

4.  "Appointments to the Regulatory Agencies," Senate Commerce Committee, 94th Congress, 2nd session (April, 1976).

# 11

## Consumerism Today: A Movement Still in Its Infancy
### Philip G. Schrag

It has become fashionable to regard the consumer movement as one that has peaked and is on the decline. Some would observe, justified by such indexes as the number of newspaper column-inches devoted to the subject, that consumerism is no longer the chic trend it was in the late sixties, having been superseded first by environmentalism and then by women's rights as the focus of attention for liberal activists. Others would claim that its goals have been achieved. Still others recognize that consumer spokesmen do not think they have achieved their goals, but argue that the movement should now recede because it has reached the point of counterproductivity; they assert that new proposals for consumer legislation will bring about results, such as higher costs, that most consumers would not support.

Viewed as a movement of an elite corps of activists, there is some truth to the observation that consumer groups are making progress at a slower rate than they once were, and that they enjoy somewhat less sympathy among many legislators and courts. This phenomenon is unfortunate, because many of the battles they have been waging are far from won. More significantly, consumer protection is potentially a far larger movement than it has ever been because continued inflation could turn consumerism into a truly mass movement; a number of important issues that have barely been surfaced by identifiable consumer spokesmen or groups could become the consumer problems around which vast numbers of people organize, with a far more powerful voice than consumer representatives now have.

## I

The needs of consumers are so diverse that people working on consumer problems today are necessarily fractionated into specialized groups, or even professions. Probably the oldest organized consumer interest is the interest in more effective dissemination of consumer information, one that has spawned the honored and important profession of home economics, whose members championed consumers long before consumerism was thought of as a movement. Similarly, Consumers Union has had a long history of bringing to large numbers of people—although hardly the masses—useful comparative price information. More recently, the advent of truth-in-lending, unit pricing, and other laws requiring increased disclosure have facilitated comparative shopping. Surely better disclosure and distribution of the information necessary for intelligent buying must be scored as one of the most impressive gains that consumers have obtained in this century.

But even here, where matters are constantly improving, we have a long way to go. The concepts of nutrient labeling and open dating of foods are still controversial. In spite of the elimination of federal discouragement, most radio and television advertisers are still unwilling to identify the inferior "Brand X" in their commercials. *Consumer Reports* reaches only a small segment of the population and is not well read by low-income groups who most need the information it contains. Many manufacturers rely on misleading reports of their self-administered testing, or confuse their consumers with dangling comparatives and half-truths.

Lehn and Fink advertised, for example, that Lysol killed germs on floors and walls, without telling people that sickness-causing germs are generally transmitted through the air, not by contact with such surfaces. Proctor and Gamble devised a television commercial claiming that "Crisco splatters 35 percent less when you're frying chicken" without telling viewers less than *what*. Anacin is said to have "the ingredients your doctor recommends" but the audience for this commercial is not told that the ingredient referred to is common aspirin. The typical advertisement is even less informative, appealing to consumers to buy a product or service because he hears a catchy tune or associates it with sex, as in National Airlines' famous "Fly me" campaign. America's major industries usually associate themselves with the concept of disclosure and consumer information, which they perceive as the least obnoxious of the goals of the consumer movement. But most of their advertising belies any genuine commitment to intelligent consumption, so over the years more and more government intervention will probably be necessary even in this least controversial area of consumer concern.

The next obvious area of consumer activism is that of product safety. We have made enormous strides since Ralph Nader wrote *Unsafe at Any Speed* nine years ago. The new Consumer Product Safety Commission is apparently very serious about its mission. Presumably it has no immunity from whatever natural law causes government agencies to become captives of the businesses they regulate, and I suppose that in five years we will have to abolish the commission and replace it with something else. But for the moment it seems to be doing a superior job. Nevertheless, we have a long way to go before we are safe from the things we buy and use. Almost every week we can read a new horror story about the dangers of additives or preservatives in food or ingredients in everyday chemical products. I have yet to see any automobile advertised as "America's safest car," which suggests that, at least as perceived by those who spend a lot of money surveying consumer tastes, safety has not yet caught on among the general public as a very important aspect of a major consumer purchase.

Next among the traditional concerns of the consumer movement I would list the campaign against fraud. Consumer agitation has produced considerable activity in this field over the last decade, and even some success. The combined attacks of Ralph Nader and the American Bar Association produced a reorganized and revitalized Federal Trade Commission, and while the commission has been somewhat less energetic in its battle against deception since the departure of Mary Gardiner Jones, not even Richard Nixon was able to disarm the FTC as thoroughly as many business organizations would have desired. Perhaps more significantly, the last decade has seen enormous growth among state and local government consumer protection agencies. Virtually every state now has either a consumer frauds bureau in the office of its attorney general, or a special department responsible to its governor, and many of these offices are armed with substantial legal power, often exceeding that of the Federal Trade Commission. But those of you who have read my depressing book, *Counsel for the Deceived*, know there is much more to preventing consumer fraud than setting up an office and enforcing a strong statute. The fact that the most serious frauds are committed by businesses that exist only for a few years makes policing the marketplace a nearly impossible task. Our legal system enables a well-represented company to drag out an investigation for more than a year, and subsequent litigation with its attendant appeals, often takes several years more. (The record, incidentally, is probably the Federal Trade Commission's 30-year battle against the Holland Furnace Company.) By the time a firm has switched lawyers three times, obtaining a postponement of the proceedings on each occasion, refused to produce subpoenaed documents, brought its own suits for millions of dollars in damages against the law enforcers personally, made countless dilatory motions, evaded service of legal papers, falsified its records, and taken numerous other steps to slow the legal process, it has made its money and is quite content to fold its shop in one state and move elsewhere. Of course, it need not do so all the time, because in many instances it can count on the sympathy of a local court, which often perceives of consumer law enforcement as the unleashing of unlimited government resources against a small, struggling businessman, when actually the battle is between a small, overextended agency and a large law firm well paid by the offending enterprise.

A small wonder, then, that serious consumer fraud is still going strong in most major metropolitan areas, particularly against the poor, who tend to complain about it less because they are more afraid of becoming involved with a government agency. At the moment, for example, we are witnessing a mushrooming of second-generation pyramid sales schemes, directed by persons who learned the business as salesmen or regional managers for the three huge national pyramids, and who have now set up their own, smaller pyramids after the authorities finally closed down the largest operations. Similarly, deception is almost as common as ever in the traditional areas of rampant consumer fraud—dance lessons, correspondence schools, English-language courses, television and automobile repair, and encyclopedia sales.

The inability of the old and new government agencies to curb traditional, old-fashioned consumer fraud has provoked the consumer movement to demand supplemental remedies. The most important of these demands is for legislation to permit consumers to file a *class action*, a suit in which one person sues not only to recover damages for himself, but for all other persons similarly situated. If a consumer wins a class action, all other consumers who were injured by the same company in the same way get their money back, even though they did not personally participate in the lawsuit.

Looking at it another way, the consumer class action takes advantage of the principle of economies of scale. Most of these frauds involve less than $500 per victim. Most consumer lawsuits involve more than $1,000 in legal work, because investigation of the facts is often extremely time-consuming. Only a fool would spend $1,000 to recover a few hundred dollars. But in a class action the duplication of effort can be avoided; the facts can be investigated and the law researched only once, although the damages may be multiplied thousands of times, depending on the number of people who were victimized.

Unfortunately, consumer class actions are permitted in only a few places, such as California and Illinois. In California, a famous class suit established that the Yellow Cab Company had been overcharging its customers. As a result of a settlement in that case, riders of cabs have been enjoying lower rates for nine years. In Illinois, Montgomery Ward was found to have violated the Deceptive Trade Practices Act by charging its credit customers for credit life insurance whether they indicated they wanted it or not. A class action forced the firm to give credits of $569,000 to 111,000 customers.

In most of the other states, courts look suspiciously on class suits, perhaps because they consume more judicial time than ordinary litigation, or perhaps because the judges believe the aggregate damages are out of proportion to the wrongdoing of the accused firms. The Supreme Court ruled last spring that in federal court class suits, the plaintiff must pay for a mailing to every member of the class before the suit can continue, thus imposing a prohibitive fee for using this device. Actually, consumers were virtually excluded from bringing their class suits in the federal courts even before that decision, because fraud is only a violation of the laws of the states, and therefore unless the Federal Trade Commission takes action, it must be remedied in the state courts.

However, Congress has the power to change this situation, and to open the federal courts liberally to all sorts of class actions brought by consumers. if Congress so acts, businesses will no longer be able to rely on the limited resources of government agencies to insure themselves pretty good odds against being sued; the amounts of money involved in class suits would make private lawyers into a new army of consumer protectors, one that would have an incentive and the legal power to pursue violators from state to state until they were brought to justice. Congressman Robert C. Eckhardt of Texas is the leading proponent of federal class action legislation, and his proposals have the support of most consumer groups, such as the Consumer Federation of America.

A completely different method of supplementing government enforcement of the laws against fraud, by vigilantism, has had some limited success in Philadelphia. There, a working-class consumer organization called the Consumers Education and Protective Associations does its own investigation of complaints of fraud, and if it finds a complaint valid it will picket the offender until redress is achieved. In return for obtaining a refund for a complainant, the organization insists the beneficiary become a member and agree to picket for others when called to do so. This group has been going strong for many years, and has done quite a lot of good in individual cases, but it has not eliminated consumer fraud in Philadelphia and, as far as I know, its efforts to export its formula to other cities have been very successful.

Closely related to the problem of fraud, which is illegal, is the problem of abusive selling practices, many of which are unfortunately still legal. The classic one, of course, is the holder-in-due-course clause inserted into the installment sales contract, enabling the seller to sell the contract for a lump sum to a bank or finance company, and stripping the consumer of his right to claim fraud, breach of warranty, or any other defense if he feels cheated and therefore stops making his regular payments. The Federal Trade Commission tentatively proposed a Trade Regulation Rule to outlaw this practice, but more than two years have now passed and the commission continues to drag its feet rather than issue the rule. Meanwhile several states have taken action, but not all of them have done so and many of the ones that have did so with exceptions and qualifications. Only Massachusetts has done away with the practice in all of its forms, including its application to sales under bank credit cards.

But the holder-in-due-course clause is only one of a very large number of harsh business practices associated with sales under contract, particularly installment sales. In Illinois, consumers are asked to sign confession-of-judgment notes; if they stop paying, they are not even notified they are being sued, much less given a chance to tell a court they had a good reason for doing so. Several states permit wage assignments, again depriving debtors of a day in court prior to their creditor's seizure of their wages. The rules regarding the sale of repossessed merchandise are lax, and a careful, empirical study in the *Stanford Law Review* has shown that their abuse, by automobile dealers acting collusively, is common.[1] Contracts frequently allow the seller to recover his lawyer's fee if he sues the consumer and wins, but the consumer is not given the same privilege. Contracts for future services often require consumers to pay long in advance of receiving what they pay for, and to lose their money if they become physically unable to use the services or if the company goes out of business. Some small-print contracts waive trial by jury, or even the right to trial by a judge, along with the consumer's warranties and other rights. Some bind a co-signer to pay for any goods that the consumer buys in the future, even if the co-signer does not know about the future sale. These and many other practices are slowly being attacked by consumer organizations; their continued existence is a measure that we have not yet experienced the "hegemony of the consumer" often touted by the media.

The consumer movement has had little success to date in reforming the courts in which consumer debts are collected, and the courts themselves are the major problem area. Professor David Caplovitz' new book, *Consumers in Trouble*, which is an empirical study of consumer debt collection in four states, documents what shabby treatment we give to debtors who are hauled into court.[2] Although the great majority of defaulting debtors are people with whom we have some sympathy, people who defaulted because of illness or unemployment or because they believe themselves to be the victims of fraud, we give them less due process than we give to criminals. A substantial proportion of them—between 20 percent and 40 percent, depending on the state—are never given notice they have been sued, because although the law requires such notice, summonses in consumer cases are frequently discarded by process servers reluctant to face a hostile consumer in a dark tenement hallway. These process servers instead file perjured affidavits claiming they did give notice to the consumer defendant, who first learns he has been sued after he has lost his case by default and his wages have been garnished from his employer.

But Caplovitz has done more than merely document the well-known abuse known as "sewer service." He has examined what happens to those people who *do* receive the summons, and has discovered they might as well have remained in ignorance of the suits against them. For in every metropolitan area that he studied, virtually all of the cases ended in default judgments against the consumer. In only 8 out of the 1,200 cases he studied did the consumer obtain a trial; those rare trials were largely the result of efforts by a particular legal aid lawyer in Chicago. Caplovitz and I have both speculated on the reasons why consumers who know they are being sued almost invariably default:

1.  Consumers who are sued are afraid of the law; many would rather pay an unjust debt than become entangled with lawyers and courts.
2.  It is very difficult to defend yourself in a regular court without a lawyer, and a lawyer will usually cost more than the amount claimed by the creditor.
3.  Summonses are very confusing. The New York summons, for instance, contains the date it was typed but not the date the consumer must appear. Many consumers see only the date that has passed and assume it is already too late to respond. The rest of the summons is a 91-word sentence followed by a 96-word sentence.
4.  In some cities, many people do not know how to find the courthouse, which is located far from any residential or commercial area.
5.  The law often allows the creditor to sue in the county in which it is located; in some cases (for example, mail orders), this is far from the consumer's residence.
6.  Our legal system often allows either party to obtain several postponements of a case just by asking for them. So a creditor's lawyer can force a consumer

to show up in court time after time, and the consumer often has to miss work or hire a baby sitter each time.

7.  The creditor can invoke pretrial discovery procedures, and make pretrial motions, which the consumer may not understand. If the consumer fails to respond to these procedures, he can lose his case by default, and in some areas of the country, he is put in jail.

8.  Many judges do not like to try consumer cases; they regard them as boring, and think they involve sums too small to justify trial time. A consumer who has jumped all of the hurdles I have listed may therefore be coerced to discuss settlement in the courthouse corridor. In such a negotiation, the consumer himself is often unrepresented by counsel but he negotiates with a creditor's lawyer who is experienced in these matters and who claims to know how the judge handles cases like these in which consumers insist on trials.

Incidentally, a Federal Trade Commission study several years ago demonstrated that retailers who sell to low-income customers resort to the collection courts far more readily and more often then do department stores selling to the general public.

Last on my list of the objectives of the organized consumer movement is improvement of institutions to which consumers can take *their* grievances, such as small claims courts. Here, too, some important strides have been made recently, but here, too, we have a long way to go. In many places, the small claims courts are open simultaneously to consumers and to creditors who are suing consumers; the far greater volume of the latter type of suit has insured that courts are primarily instruments of collection, and that the court officials, particularly the intake clerks who talk to the plaintiffs, are more sympathetic to the "regulars," the lawyers who know the court routine, than to the consumers, who do not. Even where creditors do not dominate the small claims court, consumers are often deterred from using them by their distant location, awkward and unvaried hours, and overtechnical procedure. In New York, for example, if a business is known as "Jack's Bargain Store" and advertises itself as such, you can sue it in the small claims court and if your cause is just, you can presumably obtain a judgment. But Jack's can have the last laugh, by showing long after the suit is over that its official corporate name is "Jack's Clothing and Appliance Store, Inc." Although there is no real confusion about what store you were suing, you will not be able to collect on your judgment. Of course, not many consumers who have this experience are going to be eager to use the court when they are wronged. Similarly, there is often a problem with collecting small claims judgments simply because some businesses that decry consumer "deadbeats" loudly refuse to pay. Collecting a small judgment against someone who will not pay it voluntarily can be as expensive and time-consuming as collecting a large one, or even more expensive, because the judgment will not be large enough to interest a professional collector who works on a percentage basis.

## II

The issues discussed so far—disclosure, product safety, fraud, harsh contracts, the courts and consumer remedies—have been among the primary concerns of the organized consumer movement. But an even larger number of fronts are just now being opened, and, on many of them, it looks like large numbers of consumers, rather than professional spokesmen, will do the leading. With respect to all of these new consumer issues, continuing inflation is likely to be catalytic; what used to be accepted as cause for quiet grumbling may become cause for outraged action. If this happens, the anger of consumers will be directed most strongly against high prices that can be blamed on inefficient, noncompetitive, highly concentrated industries. If the teaching of Galbraith's *Economics and the Public Purpose* is generally accepted, and the public accepts the premise that market giants such as the automobile companies, the appliance manufacturers, and the largest food companies have the power to set prices and lack incentives to keep them low, we may begin to hear demands for a very different kind of consumer protection. For Galbraith identifies the key incentive among such firms not as the profit margin, but as the maintenance of salary and prerequisites by middle and upper management.[3] If so, we may hear demands for such forms of consumer protection as regulated salaries and fringe benefits for management in major industries that cannot keep their prices down, a measure that may first be tried in overtly monopolistic industries such as public utilities and then later applied to the industrial oligopolies. Or we may hear increased talk of selective nationalization of "yardstick" companies; for example, one government-run oil company, like the TVA, used to challenge the efficiency of the others. We have never had a mass consumer rebellion, so it is difficult to predict the direction in which one might go, but it is hard to overstate how much political power consumers could seize if sufficiently aroused by a continuation of simultaneous trends in the direction of greater inflation and increased unemployment.

On a less apocalyptic level, general consumer protest is already leading the organized consumer movement into new areas. Recent rate increases by utilities have involved an unprecedented number of citizens in protests and formal opposition and have produced, in reaction, a large number of new consumer organizations. At the same time, a number of writers have attacked the federal system of rate regulation, such as supervision over airline fares, as nothing other than legalized cartelization, and spiralling rate increases cannot help but popularize their demands for major changes in these areas.

There has always been grumbling, too, about the apparently decreasing quality of many, if not most, consumer products, about how much longer things used to last. This, also, has not been an issue that organized consumer groups have been able to deal with, but as prices increase, and particularly as the cost of repairs outstrips even average inflation, the short life span of goods may become a new consumer issue.

Similarly, one of the sectors of the economy in which prices are rising most quickly is professional services, an area that has been curiously exempt from scrutiny by most consumer groups. The fantastic increase in the cost of hospital services has already led to a few radical changes in that area, and more are on the way. One of the Nader groups this year published a booklet that is a comparative guide to doctors in suburban Washington; although it brought howls from the medical groups, it is plainly an important service to publish comparative lists of professional fees and of such information as whether a doctor will make house calls, and such booklets will undoubtedly be written for all areas of the country.

In the legal profession, we strenuously oppose consumer protection; it's unethical for us to advertise, and in most areas of the country we still have minimum fee schedules (although we have never had maximum fee schedules). I suspect that within a few years, even the lawyers will have to give in to demands for change, and that as a result, prices for legal services may not rise as quickly as they otherwise would.

I have not even mentioned what is potentially the most explosive consumer issue of them all: the effect of inflation on the poor, who are apparently being hit harder than most. If you think you are having trouble coping, imagine trying to deal with our present inflation on a budget that used to allow you to eat meat twice a week and now allows you no meat at all, unless, like an increasing number of the elderly poor, you are willing to eat dog food. The poor are hardest hit because welfare benefits do not keep pace with prices as wages tend to do, and because the poor spend a larger proportion of their budgets on food, the price of which has risen faster than the consumer price index as a whole. When the middle class is itself experiencing lean times, it has the least time or sympathy for the plight of those who have less, and its members are least disposed towards proposals to redistribute income downwards.

Just imagine yourself, for instance, in the position of Claire Steere, described last May in the *Wall Street Journal* Mrs. Steere and her family of three children must live on the welfare budget of $346 a month provided by the state of Massachusetts, which is one of the more generous states in terms of welfare allowances. Welfare payments have risen by only 5 percent in the last two years, while inflation has amounted to 14 percent in Massachusetts. As the *Wall Street Journal* put it,

Cuts in the Steere's living standard are easier said than done. The family has never ventured beyond a 100 mile radius of Lowell, a grimy industrial city of 94,000 in Northern Massachusetts, so there's no leisure travel to cut. There are no liquor bills to eliminate because Mrs. Steere doesn't drink and almost never entertains. And there are no magazine subscriptions or purchases of books, records or art to be cut from the budget because they've never been part of the budget. The family can't lean on savings because there are none.[4]

The article went on to report that the Steere's house is deteriorating rapidly, but the family can't possibly afford to repair it, so the pace of deterioration continues to accelerate. And as for food,

Meat meals in the Steere household are mostly one or another variation of ground beef. Mrs. Steere makes three varieties of meat loaf and meatballs. Other dinners are bacon, lettuce and tomato sandwiches and tuna on toast. By the end of the two week period, she's serving increasing numbers of meatless dinners, like macaroni and cheese, pancakes with corn syrup or baked beans with cole slaw and bread.[5]

Welfare budgets have always been too low to support what most of us would call a minimally decent and dignified style of living, but our current inflation is making a low income utterly impossible to live on.

Yet, television, particularly through commercial advertising, continues to bring the same message of boundless affluence—of airline travel, luxury cars, and limitless varieties of appliances—to the near-poor who are becoming poor and the already-poor who are finding themselves unable, for the first time, to obtain even the barest necessities. It is all too reminiscent of the middle 1960s, when the gap between expectations and reality helped to produce the anger that led to rioting from one end of the country to the other. We tend to forget about the riots, and about the Kerner Commission's finding that the consumer grievances of the poor were among their causes. Few of those grievances have been remedied, and yet a more serious cause for grievances becomes plainer every month to those who live below the poverty level—a diminishing share of real purchasing power. This consumer problem may be so serious as to engulf all of the others. Although the scope and nature of welfare, food stamp, and other federal and state transfer programs have not traditionally been a concern for consumer and business groups, they may have to be viewed as a priority consumer issue in the relatively near future.

## Notes

1. Shuchman, "Profit on Default: An Archival Study of Automobile Repossession and Resale," *Stanford Law Review* 20 (1967):22.

2. Caplovitz, David, *Consumers in Trouble: A Study of Debtors in Default,* (New York: Free Press, 1974).

3. Galbraith, John K. *Economics and the Public Purpose* (Boston:Houghton Mifflin, 1973).

4. *Wall Street Journal* (Eastern Edition), Tuesday, May 21, 1974, p. 1.

5. Ibid.

# Discussion

*Comments:* We frequently fail to find an effective solution because we have misdefined the real problem—consider the picture of a seven- or 8-year-old child of a welfare family buying four- or five-day-old lamb chops at the supermarket. In another area, consumer groups are in one sense no different from government agencies in their inability to put themselves out of business once their mission is accomplished. In their vulnerability to losing effectiveness with the passing of time, consumer groups may be engaging in overkill in their efforts to find solutions.

*Green:* I would place remedies such as federal chartering of corporations, antitrust enforcement, and corporate dissolutions high on my list of priority goals, certainly over worrying about the performance of toasters, for example.

*Schrag:* I would place national advertising high on my list of priorities because much of the hard core fraud that exists today is permitted to continue because of the climate of thinking that national advertising has created among judges and legislators and the citizenry in general. National advertising has so conditioned us to disbelieve what we see and hear that we have little sympathy with those who do believe and are victimized by hard-core blatant misrepresentation. As a result, judges and legislators and many members of the middle class have little sympathy with the notion that anyone really believes the types of deceptions typically involved in hard-core fraud.

Consumer sovereignty as a first line of defense against fraud and deception is not a viable remedy. Some types of misrepresentation, for example, with respect to drug efficacy, cannot be detected by a consumer; and for some goods, the first purchase can be very expensive and hence the price that must be paid in order to uncover the deception is too high.

The goal is not a complete elimination of all consumer fraud but a reduction in its incidence. Consumer education will never be a real solution unless society is willing to spend "tens of billions of dollars." Since this is obviously not in the cards, I would prefer to spend whatever money is allocated to consumer deception on other types of remedies.

*Green:* Consumers receive more effective protection at the hands of courts than with legislators because of the absence of special interest pressures on courts. Also, I am convinced that the size and power of consumer groups should not be exaggerated nor should people start worrying about whether there are too many consumer groups with nothing to do. It's terribly difficult to fund these groups, to maintain their longevity; they go out of business as often as they go into business. Even the phrase "going into business" is a misnomer. It makes them sound as if they have a balance sheet and can make money. In fact, they are wholly dependent on the largesse of foundations, or on lecture fees, book royalties, or donations from public-minded citizens. I don't have any anxiety that they will pose a threat of overkill. Quite the contrary, there are not enough consumer organizations.

99

# 12

## How to Serve Consumers and Make a Profit

*James S. Turner*

The topic "How to serve consumers and make a profit" seems to contain the notion that maybe there is a dichotomy between serving consumers and making a profit. You cannot make a profit without serving the consumer. You have to do both. Much of what is wrong with our economy today is a failure to recognize the crucial, essential need to satisfy consumers or customers in order to make a profit.

There are two aspects to the way we approach dissatisfaction of the customer or the consumer. One, is to address a series of problems, specific problems, like learning about the quality of the product by being sure that it is labeled completely and informatively, that its advertising makes affirmative disclosures, and that you know what you need to know about it. Another problem is to be sure that the products do not fail. Products should in fact do the things they are expected to do. When those expectations are honestly created but your car does not start or your plane does not fly, you confront a problem of obtaining redress. In addition to information and redress you have the additional problem of correcting the underlying situation that gave rise to the problem, such as recalling an unsafe product. These are specific kinds of issues that are a part of the consumer movement.

Efforts to satisfy the consumer beget a variety of industry programs such as warranty programs, safety programs, quality control programs, labeling programs, and advertising programs. All of these steps are important, but they are only one-half of satisfying the customer or the consumer. The other half, which is equally if not more important, is to bring the consumer directly into the decision-making processes of business enterprises. This means the kind of advertising that is done can no longer remain purely the province of the advertising department of corporate enterprises. It means the kind of labeling that is done can no longer remain solely the province of the people who design labels for a living, or of the companies that order the label. What is happening? Society is now recognizing this second important aspect of satisfying customers. When you hear that California has a lot of consumer laws it is an expression of the belief that someone else—representatives of the public—must be involved in making the kinds of decisions that either anticipate, prevent, or correct the problems that occur in the marketplace.

We are in a very important kind of race at present. The race is to determine whether citizens organized as independent groups who have support financially and who have expertise are going to be able to carry out the role of defending the consumer interest in the marketplace through all kinds of private mechanisms that can be put into place. In other words, are we going to get the private-sector consumer movement that includes the people who buy involved in the decisions about what is sold and how it is sold? That is one possibility. On the other hand, there is the possibility (and it seems to be happening at the moment) that an ever increasing role for government in making these kinds of decisions will be created, particularly through regulatory agencies.

It is extremely important at this particular juncture in the development of the American economic system to think carefully about the kinds of trade-offs we make concerning what roles we assign to government. Unless mechanisms can be worked out so organized consumers can be represented by competent, trained people, such as lawyers, economists, scientists, and so forth, we are going to end up with a repeat or an expansion of the kind of regulatory system from which we now suffer. We need to develop various kinds of private, non-governmental institutions to represent the consumer interest, which can interact in the private sector's decision making about advertising, labeling, product failure, product safety, and product quality. Without these mechanisms, we will only make our problem worse, and we will lose most if not all of our national economic vitality.

If we approach our problems by simply creating or expanding our regulatory structures, we will only be taking a step backwards. The FDA, for example, has kept our food supply from sinking below an unacceptable minimum but it has not been able to move us beyond that minimum toward a better food supply. Nor will any regulatory agency ever move us from the barely acceptable toward the excellent. It will only be the interaction between consumers and producers with equal power in the marketplace where all those decisions are made that will move us towards excellence.

The way the debate about how to satisfy the consumer interest is unfolding as an issue in this society is a direct outgrowth of the kinds of economic and political decisions we as a society and as a country made over the past several hundred years. As Americans, we said some 200 to 300 years ago (our revolution began long before 1776 if you look at our history), that power grows out of the individual upward and that individuals have basic inalienable rights. This was meant to be both an economic and a political statement. When we threw the tea into Boston Harbor it was the East India Company's tea. The rhetoric that accompanied that act was anticorporate rhetoric. Whenever the East India Company got into economic trouble, it went to the King and got, or tried to get, a subsidy. We said this company is invading our rights, it is getting special handouts from the government, and we will not tolerate that.

In that very year, 1776, Adam Smith wrote the *Wealth of Nations,* attacking the interrelationship between government and corporate enterprises because it impeded the development of a free marketplace. He considered consumption the sole end and purpose of all production, believing the producer's interests should be considered only to the extent it advances that of the consumer.

We have lost sight of the basic premise upon which our entire economic system is based, namely, that our economic system will not work unless there is equality of power between producers and consumers. Without that equality of power, the marketplace begins to tilt, begins to become skewed towards one side, towards the producer's side in this instance. It begins to work in such a way that there is sloppiness on the quality side. When quality is going down and price is going up, you call it inflation. You continue that long enough and you will end up with a collapse of your entire economic system. We have lost sight of the crucial need for the consuming interest to be put in direct interaction with the producing interest so we can make sound economic decisions as an economy.

What we have done for the last 100 years is to develop very intricate, very well thought out producer institutions. When an individual goes into a supermarket today to look at a can of beans, that can of beans has a lawyer, an advertising department, a package design department, a marketing research department, and a whole range of other specialists behind it—all committed to selling, all given the task of telling us we should buy that can of beans. As individuals, we stand there on our own, representing a small economic enterprise (the average American home is larger than many small businesses), with no buying agent, no lawyer, no marketing department, no research group, nothing. We are totally alone when we make our purchasing decisions for the food we buy, the housing, the car, the appliances, the rugs, the furniture, even the mortgage. It is impossible for those 220,000,000 consumers going out and making their buying decisions to be consistently correct in making the best buy. They just do not have the time, the resources, or the capabilities to make all those buying decisions and make them correctly. Such a situation is extremely hard on the individual consumers as they watch their dollars disappearing because they cannot make the best buying decisions.

But it is even worse on the economic system because the consumer's inability to make the best buy means we have lost the discipline of the consumer in the marketplace. A very important and leading engineering consultant to industry, who happens to be a critic of the consumer movement and also a person who is trying to tell business what it has got to do in order to avoid the pressure of the consumer movement, has tried to address this problem specifically. He asserts that:

. . . the rule of caveat emptor, let the buyers beware, was a sensible rule for a period of time when you had small village economies. It forced the user to grow up and it kept the courts out of the small day-to-day transactions. The rule is still sensible wherever buyer and seller meet in the village marketplace to haggle over beans, fish, or mules, as in the villages of India, Greece, and Spain. Not only is there in these situations a near equality of product knowledge between buyer and seller but also they live in the same village. The resulting clear identity of the parties within an atmosphere of village discipline helps to keep them both honest.

Our industrial civilization meanwhile has destroyed the premises justifying the rule of caveat emptor, i.e., it has destroyed the near equality of product knowledge, the clear lines of personal responsibility and the pressure of village discipline. The small user is hopelessly ignorant of what the manufacturer did when he built the T.V. set, the tire, the automobile, and I would add food. In addition, the small user is caught in the confused inter-relationships of manufacturer, merchant, and service shops without the benefit of village discipline to keep order. The exaggerations which were once tolerable are now misrepresentations which are no longer tolerable.

Today we have a mature twentieth-century production sector and an eighteenth-century consumer sector. Unless we can build institutions of comparable strength to bring the consumer interests and viewpoints directly into the decision making of the economic structure at every level, corporate boards, corporate management, market research, legal, regulatory agencies, etc., the answer will be increasing government regulation, and increasingly inefficient operation of the economy.

There are two parts to making sure that serving consumers is profitable. We need to have the consumer protection programs of the type that many conscientious industry people are innovating. We need to be sure that every conceivable kind of innovative program relating to the rights of the individual, in terms of fair, not misleading advertising, complete labeling, warranties, product recall, and safety quality engineering, is developed.

But those programs alone will only lead us further into a morass of government intervention, into decision making that will not necessarily be reflective of what I regard as a much more vital need for consumer participation if we are to have an energetic marketplace.

The other half is that these programs must be developed by producers in conjunction with consumers. Consumers must be organized, with support, to be able to move into that decision-making area. Without an organized consumer movement, operating and having access to that marketplace, corporate decision makers and their policies will run behind the demands of the marketplace to have such policies.

# 13

## Is the Concept of Consumer Sovereignty an Adequate Index of Consumer Satisfaction in the Marketplace?

*Herbert S. Landsman*

Federated is the largest department store group in the country, with an increasingly important representation in mass merchandising stores and supermarkets. The corporate office is small, and the real merchandise professionalism resides in the 19 local and regional operating divisions in the company.

Our company has grown and prospered, and has done so by following some fundamental concepts, the most important of which is customer satisfaction. We cannot continue to grow profitably with dissatisfied customers. It just is not possible.

Every day we get a note from a customer that says: "cancel my charge account. I was treated badly in the notions department"; or "the typewriter didn't work and I wasn't satisfied with the way the account was adjusted." That is always a sad moment. Something went wrong in the system. All moral reasons aside, it hits us where it hurts: our cash register.

It is in our selfish interest—because of the nature of our department stores with cross-shopping in many departments—to treat each sale, or try to treat each sale, as an important, binding relationship with the customer. This is getting more difficult to do each day for many reasons, but whenever we fall short, it hurts us directly. The philosophy, "the customer is always right," is a sound business approach for us.

Shopping at the major department store in town is a very natural thing for local residents to do, and we have done enough customer surveys to know that there is a built-in trust factor that makes the relationship between store and customer comfortable and intimate. In a way it has made coping with the "new" consumer easier, because many Federated stores have been geared for more than a century to respond to the changing needs and life-styles of its customers.

### The New Consumer

What can we say about today's customer? Consumers of the '70's not only want quality and fashion at a reasonable price, but have far more sophisticated and discriminating tastes. They are better educated than ever before, have higher expectations of the products they buy. They are more skeptical of the product claims they hear. If their needs are not met, they know exactly how to make their dissatisfactions known. They have the time and the resources to join consumer movements, and they know they are not a lone complainer.

105

Federated is responsible for 200 million sales transactions a year, producing annual sales of close to $3 billion. Most Federated stores have a continuously increased share of the market and are the headquarters store in their trading areas. These stores cannot pull up stakes and move to greener pastures. Their future is inextricably bound to the streets where they have built their businesses.

## Consumer Loyalty

Guaranteeing customer satisfaction has created customer loyalty. Forty to 50 percent of Federated's customers visit the stores once a week, spending $20 to $30 per shopping trip. Roughly two-thirds of Federated customers shop there at least once a month, and in spite of the fact that one out of every five families changes address each year, approximately half of Federated's credit customers have held their store accounts for ten years or more.

One outgrowth of the "customer is always right" philosophy is Federated's promise that: a purchase, no matter how big or small, made by a customer in a Federated store will be consummated to the customer's complete satisfaction; we will try our best to make shopping at Federated a pleasant and rewarding experience. The customer who purchases a $1.59 pair of stockings and does not receive the service she expects and is entitled to, will certainly not be back when she wants to buy a more expensive item.

## Service and Merchandise

You all have experienced the pleasure it is to be served by someone who knows the product and who cares about you, who is friendly and efficient. You also have been served, if that is the word, by inefficient, rude, salesclerks. Believe me, it's a continual struggle to improve the selling effort.

We try to see to it that all merchandise carried will be of good quality, and offered at a fair price; that information and advertising be designed to assist the customer in making a wise and informed choice. The sheer volume of goods available has necessitated training our personnel to be better informed than ever on product attributes.

As an example of what product proliferation can mean to the retailer trying to keep up with his customers' needs, consider men's dress shirts, which once were exclusively white. Stores typically handled eight to ten different styles from two or three manufacturers. With six neck sizes and four sleeve lengths, this worked out to 192 items. Now it is not unusual to have as many as twelve styles in three colors. With neck sizes and sleeve lengths remaining constant, the number of men's dress shirts now offered is closer to 864.

## FDS is Consumer Advocate

Obviously, we need to be close to how we actually live up to our own standards. The best test is always sales, profits, repeat business. In addition, each store conducts other customer evaluations somewhat differently. Foley's of Houston, for example, has conducted an annual customer survey for more than a decade, intended not only to evaluate the store's service and merchandise, but also to elicit gripes, so problems may be investigated and rectified.

Gold Circle, our mass merchandising division in Ohio, maintains a consumer advisory board where a dozen shoppers, usually mothers who can also assess children's products, are paid to attend meetings where they evaluate the store's merchandise, policies, and personnel.

Rike's of Dayton, Ohio has a full-time consumer ombudsman who meets regularly with consumer groups to hear gripes. He has the authority to resolve consumer complaints on the spot. His primary purpose is to discover and reverse problem *trends*, rather than just resolve problems on a one-by-one basis.

During a four-week period, from August 18 to September 14, 1974, Rike's five customer relations departments (one at each branch) handled a total of 451 customer statements. The majority concerned complaints, but many were routine credit adjustments for returned merchandise; credit adjustments for the difference in price between an item sold at Rike's and elsewhere for less; and inquiries regarding merchandise deliveries. One statement was actually a compliment regarding a Rike's sales girl.

Rike's customer complaints about service ranged from being overcharged $2.00 on a pair of shoes, to being billed for merchandise not received or never ordered, to having to wait over an hour and a half for tires to be balanced. Merchandise complaints ranged from a three-piece pants suit whose colors ran when washed according to instructions, to a live $7.00 plant that died. Of this particular group of complaints, all were settled to the customers' satisfaction.

Of necessity, Federated stores must rely on the manufacturer to meet product standards required by law. That must be the first line of defense. The overwhelming majority of manufacturers do. In special cases store buyers will conduct product tests and some divisions use outside testing services, but true quality control at the retail level would create exorbitant costs to the customer. The main remedy we have used is a liberal return policy.

### Returns, Refunds, and Replacements

The general policy we've adopted is: the return of merchandise will be a simple uncomplicated procedure. Satisfaction is assured on all adjustments. The customer has a right to change his or her mind.

Plenty of mistakes are bound to occur when as many as one million people per day pass through Federated's 237 stores. We aim to keep mistakes to a minimum and to try to make sure that when errors are made, amends will be made quickly. To the extent that we can use quality control measures, train better sales staffs, work with manufacturers to resolve problems, and create new merchandising approaches that lead to better internal discipline, we can reduce mishaps to a minimum.

## Defective Products

Repair service, made available by the various stores, has eliminated eight out of ten returns or replacements on small electrical appliances. Adjustments in this area have also been reduced over the years by working with manufacturers to produce better goods and to provide better warranties.

Although adjustments have been reduced on small electrical appliances, they still remain high in other departments. High adjustments are bad news because they may mean high customer dissatisfaction. Take, for example, the furniture department. Approximately one out of every seven furniture transactions requires an adjustment, as compared to a rate of 9 percent on gifts, a department notorious for generating returns. Many Federated divisions maintain work rooms whose chief function is the repair of new furniture delivered in poor condition.

With regard to defective merchandise, it should be the burden of the distributor, manufacturer, or importer to determine whether a defective product represents a possible safety hazard, because they are in the best position to have or gain the necessary technical knowledge required in making a thorough investigation. While the manufacturer, distributor, or importer is usually in the best position to handle problems stemming from product defects, he is not always willing to do so.

As an example, Rike's purchased 250 bicycles, which were all sold the same day. Subsequently, it was discovered that structural weaknesses in the bikes could result in accidents, although none had been reported. Because the importer of the bikes refused to investigate the possibility of a hazard, Rike's felt obliged to recall all the bikes and report the situation as a possible hazard to the Consumer Product Safety Commission.

As a resposible retailer, we guarantee customer satisfaction. We also feel manufacturers must stand behind the products they produce, because it is impossible for the retailer to be the only policeman.

This subject was part of a survey in the September–October 1974 issue of *Harvard Business Review*. Forty-five percent of the business executives surveyed felt manufacturers were primarily responsible for consumer problems, while only 27 percent regarded retailers as the principal contributors to consumer problems. The remaining percentage felt service industries were to blame.

The consumer, on the other hand, blames business in general. His distrust of business' ability to police its own activities is reflected in the many new laws and regulations recently enacted. The state of California alone has 52 laws regulating the activities of retailers and the end does not seem to be in sight.

## The Future

Our own studies indicate that the amount of time spent in shopping will become an important factor in the future, as more women join the work force. While our objective has always been to have merchandise assortments presented in such a way that the customer can find what she wants quickly, without wasting time, the urgency to accomplish this will become greater as time becomes more precious.

Other studies indicate that the consumer of the eighties will be even more demanding about product performance living up to product claims. There will be greater need to test and label products for energy consumption and efficiency, and for sales people to be even more knowledgeable about the advantages and disadvantages of the products they sell.

Regardless of what the future holds, it is Federated's business to stay in business and to do what it must to satisfy the consumer, whatever his or her needs. This is our heritage and our present philosophy, and I do not see why it will not hold for the new needs of tomorrow's customer.

# Discussion

*Landsman*:  Overall, let me say this about department stores and the industry. It is a highly fractionalized industry. No one department store group does a very sizeable amount of any manufacturer's business. As headquarter stores, that would mean that of the total general merchandise, apparel, furniture, drugs, jewelry, and so on sold in that market, we would consider ourselves headquarters if we did 15 percent of the market. Unlike Campbell's tomato soup, which does I think 83 percent of the tomato soup market, our clout as an individual company broadside on manufacturers, we pursue where we can identify an important resource where we are important to them, but that's very rare. Because of what's happened to cost prices from manufacturers, we have simply gone out of key goods, brand names of the highest order.

As a normal practice today, when merchandise comes in defective, we not only send it back to that manufacturer but we also charge him for the freight, it's still costly for us to manage the paper work and the handling. On the other hand if we are dealing with a resource say like Estee Lauder, to pick an example, we have less control. Estee Lauder is a very exclusive resource whom every department store in America wants to have and who does not go into every department store. Although, we're important with Estee Lauder . . ., anything that Estee Lauder does that we don't like in terms of quality, price, delivery dates, anything else, she will simply pull the line out of the store and that might in turn cost us a million dollars and there's nothing in that case to replace Estee Lauder. That's a highly desirable line from a consumer point of view. In the case of overall manufacturer defects, it was obviously detectable ten years ago that the quality of moderate and better furniture was declining and we've all suffered from furniture being delivered with legs not put on properly and so on. We formed a committee and approached this in a very formal way—the furniture manufacturer's association. Speeches were given at the time that got a great deal of publicity. In the furniture market you're dealing with a few key, moderate to better resources. You're not dealing with hundreds of people. We really got very little from them because we weren't very important to them; even to Heritage, where we do millions of dollars. But where we can, because of the size of our business, we do something. We have great clout with dress manufacturers with whom we are important, for instance.

A great deal rests on the size of the department store business in relationship to particular manufacturers. The store is not in most cases that important. In our company where there is no central buying, each Federated store does it's own buying, and nothing is combined. So we lose the clout.

*Turner*:  The concept of the retailer is emerging in a number of very important marketing areas, or the focal point of the retailer as the battleground. If you look at gasoline stations, auto dealers, food stores, pharmacies, all of them have been involved in one way or another in either litigable or activist kind of interaction with consumers over the last two or three years. This demonstrates precisely that the retailer is the focal point.

Indeed, about three years ago we began in the food area. After the *Chemical Feast*, we pulled together a series of people who work in Washington on food issues and some from around the country and began to get inroads into the FDA. so we had some kind of token relationship there in that we met with the commissioner once a month as consumer people. Out of that group grew the concept of going to the supermarket industry, and saying to them: You're retailers; why don't you become buying agents for the consumer rather than selling agents for the product? We'll help you because we have programs and ideas and things that can be worked on. It's at that point that a consumer movement begins to take on some practical viability. For example, if there is a committee of people from the industry that recognizes the quality of furniture is deteriorating so greatly it requires meeting with the association of furniture manufacturers, you would improve the clout of such a committee if there were consumers involved in those meetings who were knowledgeable about the furniture industry and who could make the kinds of arguments that need to be made, not only from the retailer point of view but from the consumer point of view. That kind of pressure has in fact worked in a number of areas in the food industry.

However, the retail food industry effort is weak; it has barely begun. But there are some interesting beginnings of potential movement. The Giant Food program was designed to set up a committee of consumers and suppliers of Giant Food products, the consumers being representatives from every established consumer group in the Washington, Maryland, and Virginia marketing area of Giant Foods. That group established a set of principles. In this particular instance it happened to be to review all drug labeling. One of the principles was that the colors on drug labeling wouldn't say artificial color anymore. The label would give the official designation. One supplier out of six refused. We said we would make an announcement, saying congratulations to five out of six guys, the other whose name is—(giving the name) will not do this, and we think it's really unfortunate. Giant then went back and reported that to number six and number six said all right we'll put them on.

That kind of ability, to be able to bring to bear organized, informal, consumer opinion, inside mechanisms that do affect buying, is as essential as fulfilling all the efforts of a good company. Without it you have all the good guys in the world sit down in a room, all of them being producer oriented and they will not produce good consumer programs. They will produce better consumer programs than they now have, they will maybe, if they all want to do, help, do their thing for consumer a little better. But without having consumers sitting down with the technical data and the ability to analyze it and say hey, look, we know what your problem is, it's this, they will not be as good as they can be. But our problem is this. How do we bring those together in such a way to make the marketplace work? Well, what we are after is to refine the decision making so the only choice left isn't whether or not to send back a million dollars' worth of goods. I was fortunate enough to be in a supermarket at the time when Kellogg came to present it's whole new marketing program for a new sugared cereal. Now I happened to be there and raise some questions that caused the buyers to go back and re-think whether they wanted that thing in their super-market. They did, they took it finally. But at least they thought about it. There are now 14 groups around the country (National Consumer League, National Consumer Congress, etc.) that are beginning to negotiate with retailers. The other side of the coin is we are beginning to get some interest in changing the back-hauling rules of food, which the retailer and the consumer together may change. In other words, if you can enlist some economic clout behind con-sumer issues, such as retailers have, you do have a real viable chance of at least addressing important issues at this point. Without that you are in serious trouble.

*Peter Jones*: The idea of interrelation between consumer groups and industry as a way of avoiding some additional government regulation is fascinating, very appealing, and has a lot of potential. That's one thing that you'll find will move the business community. Don't assume that only through the pressure are you going to persuade. That is not the only way business is persuaded to do some-thing useful for the consumer. One grocery chain took a share of market and profit away from competing supermarkets in Washington by voluntarily intro-ducing unit pricing. No one pressured them; it was just a smart business idea.

On products for stripping down, why do you just take what you can get? You find many retailing companies as well as the manufacturers of consumer products are constantly working with the supplier to strip down, in order to get to those lower income segments of the market. That goes on all the time.

As another example, there's a lot of default on consumer credit, not all in low-income groups either. A number of the major retailers have gone into family budget counseling in their own enlightened self-interest, not only because it's helpful for the customer, but because if you can help educate people in family budgeting so they don't overpurchase on credit, you don't have the default.

One thing on government regulation: There are some areas where you just can't substitute private interface. Take the flammable fabric area, for instance. Some of the most enlightened business leaders in the country were among the leaders pushing the government to adopt tough regulations on flammable fabrics. For one reason, it costs additional money if you're going to make a fabric flame resistant and you can't do that because the American public, as price conscious as it is, won't pay that extra cost unless your competitors are required to do it, too. The same on the automobile antipollution device. Can you imagine how many extra cars any manufacturer would have sold if it alone had put the antipollution device on, and said, look what we're doing for clean air. Just pay $500 more for our model than anyone else's. That's the kind of example where you must have government regulation. More and more people in the business community are awakening to that, too.

# 14 Regulation Trends at the Federal Trade Commission
## Lewis A. Engman

As the debate over how to end inflation expands beyond corporate board rooms and government councils and spills into the living rooms and kitchens of the nation, it will be important that the public—as well as government—not be misled by the hope that there is somewhere a quick and simple solution. The current inflation draws its resiliency from the fact that it has no vulnerable and vital center. It is the product of many causes—some of them causes of causes; all of them in some respects derivative; all of them important; but none by itself likely to provide a single, simple resolution.

The inventory of targets for corrective action is long. We have short supply, excessive demand, concentrations of market power, expectations of continued price increases, government regulation that protects inefficiency and increases costs, and rampant inflation abroad undercutting foreign price competition. Unfortunately, most of the solutions to these problems have associated liabilities. For one thing, they hurt.

When people say you can cure inflation with tight money and reduced spending, one of the things those people mean is that by cutting demand you can cut production so people will be willing to work for lower wages than would otherwise be the case. As labor costs cease to rise, prices will do likewise. The trouble with relying solely on an induced economic slowdown to break the wage price spiral is that unemployment will show up a lot quicker than the break in prices. It is definitely a pay now-fly later proposition, and it contains the added inequity that a lot of those doing the paying will not be around to do the flying when the time comes.

Controls also hurt. They tend to perpetuate existing inequities, cause shortages, contribute to greater inequities since wages are easy to police (and, in fact, are almost self-policing) although prices are not, and inevitably end in an orgy of price and wage increases when they are lifted.

In addition to pain, the other thing most proposed solutions have in common is that they assume the free operation of the competitive marketplace. Inherent in the tight money and fiscal austerity approach to inflation is the assumption that if demand is lower and people are willing to work for less, some sellers will be willing and able to charge less for their goods or services or, at the very least, will not be able to charge more. It assumes, in other words, that the market is operating and that no single seller has the power to resist it. If this is not the case, the economic logic of the solution breaks down entirely, for tight money will only result in the uncompetitively priced product claiming an even greater proportion of a shrinking consumer budget.

115

# Discussion

*Questions:* What is the importance of antitrust as an anti-inflation weapon? What is the realistic feasibility of such proposals as deregulation or of Senator Hart's Industrial Concentration Act, and could FTC achieve a similar deconcentration through its trade regulation rule powers?

*Engman:* Competition—and hence antitrust—is essential to the solution of some of our current inflationary and regulatory problems. Concerning the Industrial Concentration Act, Senator Hart has done a tremendous service to Congress and the people by introducing the bill but the act as presently drafted may not contain exactly the right formula. A central essential characteristic of any such bill must be its flexibility comparable to that now contained in Section 5 of the FTC act. The process of public hearings on the bill and the testimony of foreign antitrust experts are all contributing to a healthy public discussion of antitrust. The commission is now considering a number of possible trade regulation rule proposals in the area of antitrust that would look towards more effective elimination of concentration.

*Question:* Which government programs have been effective and of benefit to society, particularly which have been designed to increase the availability of meaningful information to consumers?

*Engman:* Based on conversations with members of both the executive and congressional branches, I am convinced some deregulation is a reasonable possibility. Of greater importance is the need for public debate on these issues so the public can be clear as to the costs and benefits of different regulatory activities such as regulating new entrants into the airline or trucking industries. But all regulation should not be abolished. An example of an area requiring regulation would be airline safety.

Regarding the importance of information disclosure programs, the commission is considering a trade regulation rule that will mandate the disclosure of a great variety of information about food nutrition. The form of rules as originally proposed by staff had posed severe problems in the communicability of the information which staff proposed by disclosure, and it was returned for redrafting. I hope when the rule is published it will elicit informed comments from experts in the communications field so the rule finally promulgated will be as effective as possible in achieving its announced goals.

*Question:* Should industry be allowed to take advantage of cost increases caused by the installation of required safety or pollution equipment, for example, by tacking on an additional profit?

*Engman:* Although that's a troublesome problem, its eventual solution will lie in the degree of competition in the particular market.

118

# 15

**Evaluating Corporate and
Government Responses
to Consumer Needs**

*David F. Linowes*

## Corporate Responses

Never have so many social activist groups and agencies so diligently monitored corporate social responses to consumer needs or so articulately stated their findings and requirements. In earlier times, production of goods was the thing. To produce more and more product was the mandate understood by all. Consumption was assumed, or it was taken for granted that it could readily be created. Now there has been a shift. Consumption can no longer be assumed.

It is equally clear that the corporation's role in society has grown diverse and complex. We can no longer look to dollar profit figures alone as a measure of operating effectiveness. Because of proliferating interaction between money-making and life-style objectives, traditional gauges of corporate success are no longer adequate. A new dimension has been added, the dimension of morality and citizenship. This is not reflected on existing financial statements. Customers and society have no way of determining from a profit and loss statement or balance sheet the degree of corporate conscience being exercised by a company and its leadership. A new assessment vehicle is urgently needed, one that will give visibility to a company's response to consumer needs.

It's ironic, but frequently the worst corporate abusers of the environment and of humanity look best on their current profit and loss statements. Sophisticated analysts have always been aware that managements which neglect their machinery and equipment and do not make expenditures to train junior executives often show a higher earnings picture during the short term than is justified. In time, of course, this neglect of equipment and executive personnel training takes its toll in the operating effectiveness of the company.

In the same way, business management can show good operating profit results by ignoring the harm it is doing by dumping poisonous production waste into streams or abusing the consumer. In our present system of business reporting, we do not measure—or include in any statement prepared by management— the damage done to a stream when the poisonous pollutants are dumped into it, or to the landscape when the land is scarred and mutilated by machine-efficient stripmining techniques. Nor do we give proper reporting credit for the "good" that management does. We can no longer condone avoiding accountability for these pro and con social actions.

The social scientist, the business executive, the accountant (who is the measurement expert), and the consumer should act together immediately to

119

adopt a usable measuring and reporting device for social programs in business. Socially helpful programs can be made quantifiable for measurement and for visability.

## The Socioeconomic Operating Statement (SEOS)

There is no legitimate reason why a social audit evaluating corporate responses to consumer needs could not be prepared today along with a business organization's profit and loss statement and statement of financial condition. It could be a tabulation of those expenditures made voluntarily by a business aimed at improving the welfare of employees and public, safety of the product, and conditions of the environment. Such expenditures required by law or union contract need not be included, inasmuch as these are mandatory and thereby necessary costs of doing business.

Offset against these "pro bono publico" expenditures would be those costs of socially beneficial items that have been brought to the attention of management, and that a reasonably prudent, socially aware management would be expected to undertake, but this management chooses to ignore.

The statements themselves could be prepared by a small, internal, interdisciplinary team. Members of the team might include a seasoned executive, sociologist, accountant, public health administrator, economist, or members of other disciplines whose specific expertise would apply to a particular industry or circumstance. They would then be audited by an outside, independent, interdisciplinary team.

Ralph Nader's organizations, the United Church of Christ, Dreyfuss Third Century, Yale University, are already attempting, each in its own way, to identify and give visibility to social actions and nonactions of specific companies. Congress should enact legislation allowing companies a deduction against taxable income for net social expenditures shown on the social statement for the year, which exceed a certain percentage of the taxpayer's net worth. I would recommend that such net socioeconomic expenditures which exceed 1 percent of the net worth of a company be allowed as a full deduction from taxable income. This would be in addition to all other expense and depreciation allowances already made for these same items. Such a tax allowance would consciously assert the collective responsibility for our environmental and social problems by having government and the citizen-consumer indirectly share in the costs.

Stockholders, customer-consumers, and enlightened business executives should insist that there be no further delay in implementing a standardized reporting procedure for the social actions and nonactions of a business organization. It can be done now. To a large extent the business enterprise dominates our society. Those responsible for directing the affairs of these mammoth institutions cannot be expected to initiate and expand activities that, in their immediate impact, adversely affect the profit and loss statement, thereby reflecting adversely on incumbent management's stewardship.

The adoption of the SEOS by business would provide the following:

1. By isolating social actions from business activities, it would provide new insights into a company's responsiveness to its social obligations, useful for internal management decision making as well as for customer-consumers to assess a corporation's voluntary response to consumer needs.

2. SEOS possesses a powerful potential to provide a study base for company by company comparisons of social responsiveness within an industry. Spurred by the efforts and cooperation of professional trade associations, chambers of commerce, commerce and industry groups, and other interested parties, adoption of the SEOS pattern and philosophy by increasing numbers of companies could occur in relatively quick order.

3. Companies refusing to cooperate would be indicted as much by their refusal as by their lack of social contribution and awareness. They would be subject to strong pressures by legislators, business critics, government regulatory agencies, citizen groups, and the press. In time it could become foolhardy and costly to spurn social measurement and reporting.

I predict that before the start of the year 2000, a further giant stride will be taken. Companies will be required to prepare annual socio-economic operating budgets. These would forecast in hard, practical, dollar-supported terms what the corporation expects to contribute to society in the forthcoming year towards its responsibility to the consumer.


## Regulatory Agencies

Consumerism, the new force in society, cuts across private and public sector lines. We must now ask ourselves not only whether the corporation is responding to consumer needs for what it furnishes, but whether government is responding to consumer's needs for what it furnishes. Included in the things government provides are watchdog service agencies such as the Federal Trade Commission, Food and Drug Administration, Interstate Commerce Commission, Federal Aviation Administration, and Civil Aeronautics Board. But, how effective are they?

Senator William Proxmire of Wisconsin in introducing a bill to abolish the Interstate Commerce Commission, stated:

There are more whiskers and cobwebs at the ICC than any other place in the government. With fierce competition among air, rail, barge and road transportation, regulation for other than safety purposes has long been unnecessary. The answer is abolition plus strong enforcement of the antitrust laws.[1]

The kind of human needs for which government regulatory agencies exist
and are found wanting include the Food and Drug Administration's delay on
safety rules for x-ray machines and laxity toward dangerous toys; the Transportation Department's tolerance of rickety school buses; the Commerce Department's failures in adequately restricting fire-prone clothing; and the Civil Aeronautics Board's looseness in insisting something be done about luggage handling.

Regulatory agencies of government are not the only public institutions that
come up with less than superior performance when attempts are made to evaluate them. As a matter of fact, in the public sector, most evaluation of responses
to consumer needs by government is essentially a football game played by politicians who are "out" and trying to get "in."

Under such circumstances, any evaluation of government agency and program performance is at best heavily biased, and not very constructive. Occasionally a taxpayer group or press reporter sounds off about a particular agency's
failures, but the critique soon dies down and is lost in the news of the latest
police shoot-out. As a practical matter, therefore, government responses to
taxpayer-consumer needs is hardly ever evaluated in a meaningful way.

## Government Responses

In many public agencies administrators often get mixed up in their objectives.
Several years ago as a consultant to the secretary of the Department of Health,
Education and Welfare, I learned that an agency of the department which
received massive sums of money to improve the health of children never determined whether its activities accomplished what it was charged to do. The administrator knew the number of medical checkups given, but he simply did not know
whether the children's health improved. The agency did not have a built-in procedure to make this determination.

Largely because of this lack of appropriate accountability and evaluation
machinery, many education institutions are diploma mills, many correction
institutions are cell blocks, many poverty agencies are food and shelter distributors, and some regulatory agencies are "captives" of the industries they regulate.

In the public sector, to set consumer needs-related goals and evaluate results
properly, we must apply qualitative standards of performance. We know how
many housing units are built to replace slum dwellings; but we do not know if
the slum-dweller's lot has been improved. We know what our prison population
is, but we do not know how many prisoners are being rehabilitated. We measure
the number of policemen on the force, but now how safe our streets are. We
pour billions each year into education, but we do not try to relate the increased
sums we are spending to how well our young people are being educated.

The objectives of our social institutions are confused because we operate only with quantitative standards. Yet, there is no need to operate under quantitative standards alone; qualitative standards are available, but they are not being used as part of the budgetary and control process.

Educators and sociologists are able to determine the level of reading, writing, or arithmetic achieved by a youngster, as well as the level of social development. Penologists have standards for ascertaining when a former prisoner has been rehabilitated.

It has been said that increasing the number of policemen does not prevent crime, that we do not even know what causes crime or why people commit it. Yet, police departments are evaluated for effectiveness by the number of criminals apprehended, and their budgets are directly related to the number of personnel on the staff, without consideration for whether the causes of crime are even being identified and attacked.

America's public education budget increased 1,000 percent from about $6.5 billion in 1947 to $68 billion in 1969. If costs continue to climb as they have in the past, predictions are that spending on education could eventually equal the entire gross national product.

## Set Up Social Profitability Audits

When billions of dollars of public funds are invested in social programs the public and its elected representatives are entitled to a qualitative evaluation of how the funds are being applied.

An important tool to accomplish such an evaluation is by means of a socioeconomic performance audit. Such an audit is the continuous assessment and reassessment of social performance: to insure, first, that needs have been properly defined; next, that goals have been formed in response to these needs; finally, that goals are being met as projected and on schedule.

Financial audits are accepted and effectively used in all sectors of activity—business, government, non-profit. Also, many of these same organizations use management audits to examine the efficiency with which the various functions are being executed. Now we need socioeconomic performance audits for our government agencies to verify whether the resources put into a program are directed towards the true objectives of the program.

Before determining that the job is done right, it is essential to determine that the *right* job is done, that the right need has been focused upon, that the right goal has been met. This is the role of the socioeconomic audit. The central focus is on the responsiveness to real human needs, on opportunities and deterrents.

Historically, in the social sector program, action response has been stronger to symptoms than to studied human needs. In an explosive environment, something is always done. More police are provided, more money is pumped in, more beds are made available, more guards are hired, more handouts are doled. But at best, crash action produces no more than temporary solutions, if indeed "solutions" is the word at all.

The socioeconomic performance audit, properly designed and built into the system, deals with underlying causes. It delves to the root of problems, seeks to determine why men perform as they do, and what can be done to make them more effectively respond to taxpayer-consumer needs. It thus prevents crises from erupting.

## Create Visibility

"How are we doing?" The question is posed repeatedly in the modern business establishment, day after day, week after week. Performance reports provide the answers.

Too often these answers are not provided on the government. How many welfare recipients are being made self-sufficient? How many children's reading skills are being boosted to an acceptable level? How many ex-convicts are being employed in socially acceptable jobs? We simply do not know. We do know if the lot of the disadvantaged is being improved at a rate sufficient to cool the desperation and frustration that impels men to riot. We are confused by an overabundance of numbers, and some people may even be deluded into believing that numbers are answers. Numbers are data. But they are not necessarily information. They are not always intelligent. As far as funding is concerned, they quite often may be misleading.

Witness this exchange at the higest levels of government:

*Mr. Califano of the White House Staff:* In late 1968 I asked the appropriate Government agencies how the 10-million figure (10-million hungry persons) was developed. I was told by the then Secretary of Health, Education and Welfare that what they had done was to take a rough estimate of the number of people who were poor, figured about 2-million of the adults were actually hungry, multiplied that by 4-1/2 to get a family figure, and that is where they got 10-million people.
*Senator Mondale:* It was a complete guess, wasn't it?
*Mr. Califano:* That is correct.

The above has been excerpted from testimony given at a Senate subcommittee hearing in 1970.[2] It is a shocking indication of the way vital social information is developed in this nation and made known to the public.

Yet, we must have creditable information if we are to evaluate government's response to consumer needs. The public should have it. Elected officials, budgetary authorities, boards of trustees, and the social administrators themselves should have it. If it is lacking, how can we properly appropriate billions of dollars of the public's money for hunger relief, health care, education, crime control, and all the rest?

Scores of social reformers in and out of government strongly believe that economic reports no longer suffice. Social reports are needed to accompany and supplement them at all levels of social enterprise from the federal government to the rural township. Social progress—or lack of progress—should be made known to the public and picked up by the press.

Social institutions that exist only to serve the public should certainly respond to this need for fuller and more meaningful reporting. It is long overdue.

A system of social reporting similar to our system of economic reporting would reply to the taxpayer-consumers' needs to know. Our economic indicators and reports, while far from perfect, have been highly effective in helping to plan economic strategy. We now need to give visibility to quality of life indicators for our nation in order to enable our government officials to properly respond to consumers' social needs.

Ultimately, it will be public need and public demand that will establish the socioeconomic audit as an essential and acknowledged strategy for government service consumer responsiveness. Already the pressures for increased and more effective visibility are being felt from all quarters of the public sector. Hence, the inevitability of the socioeconomic performance audit, itself, an inevitable prelude to improved visibility.


## Conclusion

In summary, I have addressed myself to the evaluation of responses to consumer needs from the corporation on the one hand and from the government on the other.

For the corporation, I suggest that business now adopt a third dimension of reporting, one that identifies and gives visibility to its social actions and nonactions. A statement such as the socioeconomic operating statement would fill this need. Such an exhibit would be prepared periodically, along with the profit and loss statement and statement of financial condition.

For government, I suggest that for all social agencies, dollar reporting is not adequate. Every financial report should be accompanied by a qualitative report of what has been accomplished. Many qualitative measurement standards already exist in the fields of sociology, psychology, and education. We need to learn to apply them to our budgetary and control processes. Further, nonprofit organizations should have regular socioeconomic performance audits. These are independent examinations of the operations of a welfare agency, a prison, a school, a regulatory agency to determine whether real consumers' needs are being satisfied by that particular institution or agency.

**Notes**

1. Congressional Record, Aug. 1, 1975, p.S14801.

2. Hearings before the Special Subcommittee on Evaluation and Planning of Social Programs of the Committee on Labor and Welfare, U.S. Senate, 91st Congress, Washington, D.C., Dec. 18, 1969.

# Discussion

*Linowes:* Profit and loss statements are still prepared and relied upon even though they are filled with ambiguities, inadequacies, and subjective evaluations. For example, the typical balance sheet does not provide any clues to the value of the results of a company's payment valuations or the value of its executive hierarchy.

A comparable lack of precision, therefore, should not prevent companies from trying to evaluate their own social performance. We need to give as much visibility to a company's social performance as we give to its financial performance, recognizing, in both instances, the very subjective basis used in selecting and quantifying the various indicators relied upon.

The need for social accounting—for putting a value on the benefits achieved through lower pollution, safer working conditions, and fewer product-related injuries is widely recognized but so is the difficulty of assigning some dollar figure to those benefits.

# 16

**An Appeal to Tired Activists:
A Radical Looks at the
Consumer Movement**

*Richard C. Edwards*

Buried in all the publicity about inflation and the economic crisis, the consumer movement limps along. From time to time, as in the vinyl chloride case, activists and consumer organizations score a direct hit. The scandalous conditions uncovered by the research are reported in the *Times*, Nader or one of his lieutenants appears before the appropriate congressional committee, and once again it appears that the corporate mighty will be humbled.

But gaining attention and support is an increasingly difficult job. Those now-rare investigations, which do attract attention more than anything else, evoke a nostalgia for the good old days, when the consumer movement seemed the wave of the future.

The present reality of the consumer movement is, unfortunately, much bleaker. The consumer research organizations report great difficulty in recruiting new investigators. Consumer activists are largely ignored, as the exclusion of Nader and other leaders from Ford's economic summit conference symbolized. Consumer organizations are largely out of money, since the foundations and public have ceased providing funds.

More ominously, consumers' issues are increasingly being defined by the well-funded and slick consumers affairs bureaus of the large corporations, along with the ponderous but timid federal and state consumer agencies. Loss of ability to define its own issues represents the final stage of impotence and co-optation.

What went wrong? Is the consumer movement destined to die, as did the civil rights or student power movements? More importantly, what can be done?

## What is the Basic Consumer Problem?

To understand what went wrong, we must go back to the basic consumer issues. We know much about the specifics: shoddy merchandise, like clothing that falls apart or telephone service that hinders rather than facilitates communication; dangerous products, like cribs that burn up; processed foods with carcinogenic additives; automobiles that fail in emergencies; false advertisements that persuade unsuspecting people that good health or cures of arthritis or old age are

William Connolly and James Crotty provided valuable comments. However, the views contained in this chapter are those of the author alone.

available for purchase; overpricing of goods, like that resulting from the electrical companies' price-fixing conspiracy, which produces huge profits, like those perennially enjoyed by the drug companies; manipulation of the consumer through the use of worthless guarantees, false claims for a product's efficiency, or hidden contract clauses; "third-party" effects, like those deriving from automobile pollution of the air or the dangers of radiation from nuclear power plants; the misuse of the public's resources, like the spoiling and pillage of public lands in the oil companies' search for shale oil and soft coal. The list could go on, but we all know the wide range of specifics.

If these are the specific manifestations of consumer problems, the general nature of the problem can be stated more succinctly; these problems are the antisocial consequences for the consumer of the normal operation of a market economy, that is, of capitalism. Normal operation is "normal" in the sense that in the absence of powerful correctives, these consequences occur.

Many consumer activists would agree with this general statement of the consumer's problem, and it certainly is supported by the attempts of the consumer movement to build institutional mechanisms, that is, agencies which will work day in and day out on a routine basis, to counteract the antisocial consequences of the normal operation of a market system. Nonetheless, some might still object. I want to defend this statement of the problem, not directly, but rather by an evaluation of the options open to the consumer movement itself.

## Three Models of Consumer Movement Intervention

In looking at the consumer movement, we might ask, what are the possible ways in which such a movement might succeed in ameliorating the antisocial consequences of business we are all so familiar with? There are basically three that have been widely considered.

The first model, what we might term the "community of interests" model, is based on the assumption that these antisocial consequences are not especially the result of any fundamental conflict of interests between consumers and businesses. Rather, they result from business's failure to understand the consumers' needs or perhaps its failure to appreciate all of the consumers' needs.

The solution to these problems, according to the "community interests" model, is that we need more communication. Perhaps we need some lobbying and arm twisting with business leaders to convince them of the seriousness of these problems. Then they will respond and change their ways. They will give us safe products, they will quit overpricing, they will quit trying to manipulate the consumer, and so on.

There is only one problem with this model: there *is* no community of interests on most of these issues between the business producers and the consumers. Businesses make profits on overpriced, shoddy, and hence unsafe goods; witness the profits of the drug companies, or of the electrical manufacturers, or of the automobile companies, all of whom historically have been dependent on producing and selling overpriced, unsafe, and unreliable goods. Businesses reduce costs (and hence increase their profits) when they ignore their impact in polluting the air or water; the impressive new refinery capacity being built in the Carribbean is in large part due to the lack of environmental restrictions (as well as tax breaks). Businesses make profits by strip mining the public lands and despoiling forever our natural heritage; witness the frenzy with which lignite leases are being bought up in North Dakota and Montana. Businesses make profits by providing worthless warranties or warranties with impossible obligations on the part of the buyer, not only because these warranties help sell the goods initially but also because if the business honored them later, they would increase the firm's costs.

The conclusion to all this is that, except on trivial issues, there is no community of interests between the consumer and business. Business's interest is to make money. A fast buck is no different than a "respectable" buck, except that it is earned quicker.

There is a variant of this theme, which says although it may be true there is no community of interest between the shady or fast-buck businesses and the consumer, nonetheless "respectable" or "responsible" businesses do not behave this way. There is a difference between "bad" companies and "good" ones, and the job of the consumer movement is to make the "bad" ones act more like the "good" ones. If only more companies would be "responsible"!

The difficulty with this approach is in identifying the "good" companies. Since the largest 200 companies now control nearly two-thirds of the manufacturing assets in this country, it is a serious problem for the "good" company argument if these big companies do not count as exemplars.

The final refuge of this argument is that although it is perhaps true the biggest corporations are involved in a lot of anticonsumer shenanigans, nonetheless smaller, local companies are "responsible." But one of the more recent consumer scandals comes from New York, where Saks Fifth Avenue, Bergdorf Goodman, and Bonwit Teller—three high-class firms—were accused of a long-term conspiracy to fix prices on retail garments. For me, the final blow had already fallen when it was disclosed that the terribly respectable and high-priced family-owned food store in Cambridge, Massachusetts—Savenors, where Julia Child has for years bought her meat—not only weighed the meat you bought but also the heavy iron hook on which the meat hung.

The point of all of this is that there are not "good" companies and "bad" ones, but rather all companies are trying to make as much money as possible. That is what they are in business for, and to expect them to do anything different is to misunderstand their nature. Doing "goods" in the world, as for example acting "responsibly" towards consumers, costs them profits. If they are very big, and have lots of profits, they may decide to do some "good works," but when it comes to seriously eroding their profits, they cannot afford to.

## Building Consumer Institutions

The second model of consumer intervention, what we might call the "institutional" model, is more realistic than the first in that it admits there exists a fundamental conflict between businesses and consumers and that "communication" or reliance on "good" companies will not help. It is admitted that what is required is power.

The solution proposed by this model is also simple: build institutional mechanisms that will protect the consumer interest and defend the consumer in the conflict between consumers and business. This solution at least addresses itself to the real issue: that of the basic conflict of interests and of the power needed to defend the consumer interest.

This model is not, however, very original. The idea of regulatory commissions, of an antitrust department of government, of all sorts of public agencies to defend the public interest against the business interest, has been tried before. Past efforts are almost a universal complete failure. Not only have such agencies failed to be vigorous in the pursuit of the public interest, they have worked in the direction to defend the very groups they were supposed to regulate. They have become federal protectorates.

As has been well documented in such books as Mark Green's book *The Monopoly Makers* or Joseph Goulden's *Monopoly*, regulatory agencies have little chance of succeeding in any meaningful encroachment on the interests and operations of big business. These agencies, to the extent they are not captured outright by their client industries, are engaged in a political struggle with business—a struggle in which they are armed with legal tools but the so-called regulated industries are armed with real political resources: money, contacts, the ability to mobilize voters in key congressional districts, finances to undertake long court suits, friends elsewhere in government, and so on.

The result is that the CAB protects the established airlines from competition: the FCC keeps new technology from eroding the monopoly position—and profits—of the three networks; the ICC helps the railroads get rid of public passenger service—and public passengers; the antitrust division sees that new monopolistic concentrations of power, such as ITT, are not prosecuted and old concentrations are left alone; and the FTC contents itself with requiring Profile Bread to alter its ads, while, as its own staffers recently admitted, potentially significant cases like the antitrust suit against the major oil companies die for lack of sufficient investigatory power.

Yet this vision of the experts selected by their professional credentials sitting in Washington regulating things for the public interest dies hard. Our belief that this is a technical problem, best left to top-flight economists or other people who "really" understand what's going on rather than a political problem involving power is too deep to be exercised easily.

In the same book (*The Monopoly Makers*) in which Mark Green and others detail in very persuasive case studies the failure of agency after agency to regulate in the public interest, the authors propose as remedy simply a new variant of the "institutional" mode.[1] Green proposes that there should be "at least one economist as commissioner in every agency" and a cabinet-level officer over all regulatory agencies, as though the old institutions did not work for lack of an economist, and some fiddling with the structure will fix things. The lessons from the overwhelming body of historical evidence are pretty hostile to this second model.

## Aroused Citizens

The third model, what we might call the "aroused citizenry" model, gets even more realistic. It starts from the premise that the problem is one of fundamental conflicts of interest between business and consumers, and the consumer can only be defended by, and this conflict can only be arbitrated by, power.

This model goes on to assume that while regulatory commissions and other agencies may be the *mechanism* for implementing the consumer's or the public's interest, the agencies cannot fight by themselves. That is, in the political process these agencies inevitably lose. Consequently, something else is needed to insure sufficient power to force the agencies to implement correct policies. That extra ingredient is the aroused citizenry, or in this case, aroused consumers.

The solution proposed by this model, then, is to build a base of public support that will pressure business, monitor, and give backbone to the public institutions enforcing consumers' interests, and in general act as the power base from which consumers can do battle with the big corporations, using from time to time the instrument of public regulatory mechanisms as well as public campaigns and other tactics.

While this model is more realistic, it also is flawed. The problem is that it is almost impossible to keep such a movement alive. Sooner or later the aroused citizenry develops other concerns, and the shocks of the original scandals, the fervor of the original meetings, dies down. This is indeed the attraction of the "institutional" model, since the building of institutions means that when the movement "cools out," there are institutions left to take up the slack.

We see this cooling out happening in the consumer movement itself, as people become more concerned with inflation, unemployment, and the prospect of depression, and lose interest in working on campaigns to improve the safety or quality of goods. It was with good reason that consumer representatives were largely excluded from Ford's economic summit—the people putting on that show realized the public is not now so concerned about traditional consumer issues, and it was politically feasible to ignore consumer groups. We see this cooling out in the failure of the Congress to pass the bill to create the Consumer Protection Agency. We certainly see this cooling out process at work when we look at the histories of other movements—the civil rights movement, the ecology movement (remember "Earth Day?")—and unless the consumer movement is something new under the sun, it is not possible to keep an aroused citizenry aroused. It is sensible that this is so: people have their lives to get on with, and they have many concerns, only one or a few of which are touched by the consumer movement.

## Other Problems

If none of these models of how consumerist groups should gain their goals seems satisfactory, it should not be thought that the problems confronting an effective consumer movement end there. Other problems also undermine the efficacy of the movement.

First, other problems exist in our society—problems the consumer movement cannot and probably should not attempt to deal with. A partial listing would include the following: persistent poverty and growing inequality, racial discrimination and racial oppression, the unequal sexual division of work and of privileges, the quality of education and the openness of educational opportunity, the exploitation of migrant laborers and other unorganized workers, ecological and environmental issues, world hunger and the economic exploitation of poor countries by the rich ones, problems of law and equal administration of justice, workers' alienation from their jobs and their demands for more control and say over their work lives, issues of health and safety at the workplace, prison reform and prisoners' rights, to name but a few.

The presence of these problems means that other movements ("pressure groups") exist to implement reforms in these areas. It is not surprising that the consumer movement has attracted mostly middle-class or higher income whites, in spite of the fact that poor people and black and brown peoples often get the most overpriced, most shoddy merchandise dumped on them. Nor is it surprising that consumer activists, sensing that they must broaden the scope of their issues if they were to retain support, have moved into several of these other areas of concern. Whether consumer types, with their middle-class origins and legal orientation have leadership to offer blacks, the poor, or prisoners remains to be seen.

Thus, to speak of "consumers" as a group or movement is misleading; what the term really means is those people for whom issues of the quality of consumer goods and the terms of the consumer transaction can be made their first priority. But most people have other priorities, and well they should—the list above of things in our society needing reform is long and pressing.

Second, it is not just that these other groups or interests or priorities exist, but that they are often in conflict with the consumer movement. For example, it is not clear that it is in the interests of poor people to pay higher taxes to support new regulatory efforts. It is not even clear that it is in their interest to see better quality and safer goods—because nearly without exception, in this corporate world, such goods are more expensive. Of course, it would be in their interest to have better quality goods at the *same* price they pay now, but when has that happened? Auto safety standards are perhaps the outstanding example of price increases resulting from consumerist activity.

It is certainly not clear that the consumer movement is in the interests of poor people when we learn that not only do past regulatory efforts require higher taxes to pay for the regulatory commissions, but these commissions wind up having *perverse* effects: poor people are presumably paying a heavy share of the $16 to $24 billion per year that Mark Green estimated results from the inefficiencies caused by just four agencies alone: the ICC, the CAB, the FMC, and the FCC. Poor people in this country do not need more of this kind of help, and what assurance do they have that the miserable track record of these agencies—not so different from new institutions consumer leaders are proposing—will not be repeated and multiplied?

Third, we now see the spector of a huge disaster for consumers—not only those who can make consumer issues their number one priority but all consumers—in the form of serious depression with high unemployment and high inflation. Moreover, there are legitimate concerns that this might be a world-wide, that is, a capitalist-worldwide, disaster.

Consumers will be concerned not about the quality of goods but whether those goods will be available at all. The capitalist business cycle, which was seemingly stamped out in the sixties, is now coming back to haunt us. The relevant point here, of course, is that when times get tight, traditional consumerist issues get lost.

The fourth issue is simply the implicit view of life as consumption, which is contained in the consumerist perspective. It borders on an acceptance of the classical and double-edged capitalist promise: accept the division of your waking hours into life, on the one hand, when you live and express the meaning of your existence, and work on the other, when you earn an income to support your nonwork life. But what about meaningful work? What about living life and being a meaningful member of one's community *through* work rather than just outside of or in spite of work? What about the possibilities for human growth and development by an integration of, rather than a separation of, one's worklife and one's "real" life, one's producing activities, and one's consuming activities?

## The Underlying Unity of Protests

It should be noted that the problems raised above are not the entire range of problems that a "state of the consumer movement" evaluation would consider.

For example, I have not touched on specific organizational issues, questions of tactics, fund raising, and so on. Instead, all of the problems described are simply those that derive from an unfortunately all-too-common assumption that the consumer movement is and ought to be an independent, separate movement.

The fundamental fact underlying all consumer issues, that is, underlying the antisocial consequences of the normal operation of a market economy, is the fact of corporate power. Capitalist corporations wield enormous power, and their power is largely beyond the reach of any democratic social control.

But this power also underlies the problems faced by those other groups mentioned: it is one of the biggest barriers to overcoming racial and sexual discrimination, to ending poverty and inequality, to eliminating the stultifying and meaningless character of work, to the economic exploitation of poorer countries, to the oppression of migrant workers, to resolving the accelerating damage being done to our natural environment, and so on.

So we notice immediately that the fundamental target of all those movements—and the consumer movement—ought to be the same: the undemocratic and antisocial nature of corporate power.

Moreover, the fatal flaws in all three of the models of consumerist intervention described above can be traced precisely to their failure to undertake a serious program to undermine the power of corporations. The "community of interests" model denies that power is an issue. The "institutional" model and the "aroused citizenry" model both seek to counter corporate power, but not to undermine it.

The issue then is whether we are going to be serious about bringing this power under some kind of democratic control.

## What Is the Nature of Corporate Power?

The power of corporations comes in many forms. It is political influence in Washington, and even more so in state and local governments, and in both major political parties. It is the power to influence public opinion by advertising, buying media time, presenting information, and so on. It is the power to undertake lengthy, expensive court cases to delay, tie-up, or otherwise subvert threats to their operations. But in the end these are not really fundamental. The fundamental power that corporations have is the power to invest.

The importance of this power can be thought of in the following way. Society produces a certain amount of goods and services every year. A portion of that is required simply in order to feed, house, and maintain the population, to replace those tools and factories used up in production, and so on. These are the necessary expenses of producing those goods and services.

What is left over is a surplus—to be used as society sees fit. It is this part of society's produce over which the society has options. In ancient Egypt, the surplus was used to build pyramids. In the Middle Ages, it was used to build cathedrals and support crusades. In capitalist society the surplus accrues primarily as profits, and, of course, it is over profits that the corporation has control. The power to invest, then, is in reality the power to dispose of society's surplus.

Let me list some examples showing how this power to invest society's surplus has had fundamental consequences in shaping the world we live in:

1. The decision to invest in automobiles rather than public transportation systems, thus establishing basic parameters for the subsequent development of housing, of transportation, and of cities;
2. The decision to mechanize cotton-picking in the South, thus eliminating the basis for southern blacks' role in the rural economy and necessitating their migration to northern cities;
3. The decision to intrude our economic system and interests into the economies of underdeveloped countries, setting up a new economic system of colonialism;
4. The decision to relocate industry outside the central city, thus destroying traditional neighborhoods, making slums of our cities, and increasing the blight of suburbanization;
5. The decision to relocate industry from New England to the South and Southwest, imposing on New England's workers the burden of being unemployed and obsolete;
6. The decision to build factories outside of midwestern farm areas, thus depopulating many of the farming communities of the Midwest and attracting the young people away to the cities
7. The decision to invest in work and production technologies that are ever more degrading and stultifying to the workers and that inhibit the possibilities for effective worker control over work and participation in decision making;
8. The decision to undertake strip mining, to invest in production plants that pollute the air and water, to build potentially catastrophic nuclear generating plants, and so forth.

All these tremendously important decisions were made by private corporations, exercising their power to invest. They did not make these decisions arbitrarily, of course; they made their decisions because they thought their investments would yield high profits. Neither can we say these decisions were not somehow "good" or "progressive" in the long run; many of them were or might still be.

But, still, two points remain: They were decisions of fundamental importance to our society, taken without concern for the tremendous human costs involved, that is, without even minimal cognizance of the antisocial consequences accompanying them. They were fundamental decisions affecting the lives of most people in which the broad masses of people in this society had no effective voice.

The conventional response is, of course, the economists' notion of "consumer sovereignty." Surely the profits those firms reinvested have been earned only because the companies satisfied consumers' desires.

But the market is only one of many social decision mechanisms, so it must be evaluated in terms of the rightness or wrongness of its decisions. I want to suggest some arguments to the effect that market decisions are fundamentally undemocratic and hopelessly biased towards decisions that are individually rational (given the irrational character of the world in which the decision must be made) but socially disastrous.

The market mechanism, first, bases its determination on an unequal and antidemocratic distribution of the "dollar votes." It may be trite, but must never be forgotten, that the preferences of a person with an income of $100,000 receive ten times the weight of the person with a $10,000 income.

Moreover, the market mechanism, by forcing consumers to act as isolated individuals, often excludes alternatives more preferred by consumers as a group. I, like many, accepted the II-S draft deferment during the 1960s as a personal solution to an irrational and unfair system. Yet, I would have strongly preferred a system in which inequitable loopholes were eliminated. In the case of the draft, it was possible to "vote in" a new system. But it is only by going outside of the market economy that it is possible to express a collective preference for mass transit rather than automobiles, or a clean environment rather than wasteful industrial growth.

Who expressed a preference for the sprawling blight of suburbanization, little shared space or facilities, and the decay of all major center cities? Given that there was no mechanism for intelligent and humane community planning, it was of course "rational" for "sovereign" consumers to choose the individual solution of a suburban home. Hence we wind up with a pattern of residential (and industrial) location that is socially irrational, probably against the preferences of consumers had they been able to express those preferences in a collective fashion, but often cited as the "true" preferences of consumers by virtue of their revelation in the marketplace.

Who cast the "dollar votes" for crowding the black population into urban ghettos? Who cast the "dollar votes" for investing in alienating, boring, and nonparticipatory work technologies? Who cast the "dollar votes" for pollution, strip mining, or potential nuclear disaster?

Further, any familiarity with the operations of modern corporations must create a healthy skepticism of the purity of consumer preferences in a world where corporations spend roughly $25 billion a year (in direct expenditures only) to convince the consumer of what he or she wants.

Finally, and perhaps most importantly, the market precludes the large educational benefits that might derive from collective discussions of the impact of consumption alternatives. How many more persons would have become concerned about the destruction of the environment or the human costs of relocating industry away from the center city had there been a political, rather than impersonal and largely invisible market mechanism, for making social choice?

Consumer sovereignty seems a weak force to counterpose to the power of the corporations. Until the corporations' power to invest is brought under social control, that is, made accountable democratically to the people, the "antisocial consequences of the normal operation of a market society" will continue.

## Where Does All This Leave Us?

Where do we go from here, or more precisely, where can the consumer movement go from here?

One option is that consumer activists can decide to go it alone, contenting themselves with making marginal adjustments at great effort for themselves and at some cost to other groups in society. Where "common interests" between businesses and consumers exist, consumer groups will "facilitate communication." There can continue to be a fascination with ideas like putting one economist on every commission and regrouping agencies, and consumer groups can have conferences to convince themselves that their enthusiasm and support will last as long as there are corporations still interested in turning a fast buck.

The other option is to join with all those other groups—and hopefully many more than exist now—who are trying to achieve democratic control over society's economic resources: those groups who are trying to vest the power of deciding how society's surplus gets used in the only appropriate group, namely, all of society, rather than in a priviledged and self-interested minority.

Joining up with this more widespread social movement would not for consumer activists mean losing their focus on consumer issues. As we all know from the effective work done by consumer groups over the past few years, these are explosive and important issues, and they have the potential for mobilizing many people. Rather, joining up means raising those issues in the context of the *whole* change required in order to achieve a decent and humane society. That change, as I have argued, is ending capitalism.

I do not mean to suggest that there is a "blueprint" for society that can immediately be instituted to achieve democratic social control over our economy. The actual, practical institutional forms required must be worked out by people and groups struggling to implement fundamental change, and in so doing, developing appropriate institutional forms. Any other "blueprint" is immediately suspect.

Nonetheless, the task before us seems straightforward, even if staggering in its dimensions:  we need to put socialism on America's agenda for the 1970s. It needs to be a socialism based on the principle that democracy must be extended to our economic institutions. It must be a socialism in which power is rooted in decentralized, community control over economic resources. In short, it must be an American brand of socialism, expressly tailored for the democratic possibilities and experience of our people. But within that context, the potential for creating a truly decent society is immense.

## Note

1.  Mark J. Green, (ed.) *The Monopoly Makers* (New York: Grossman Publishers, 1973).

# 17

## A More Traditional View of Public Policy and the Marketplace in Meeting Consumer Needs

### Richard D. Murphy

The FTC's Bureau of Economics enjoys a close working relationship with the Bureau of Competition, the agency's antitrust arm. Staff economists regularly aid the antitrust lawyers in selecting cases, identifying key economic issues, and fashioning effective relief. Unfortunately, the path between the Bureau of Economics and the Bureau of Consumer Protection is somewhat less well traveled. In truth, commission economists have barely begun to develop the analytical tools and personnel necessary to tackle a regular scrutiny of the social costs and benefits of proposed trade regulation rules and deceptive practices litigation. I was fortunate enough to be asked by the bureau's director, Dr. F. M. Scherer, to assume responsibility for improving our capabilities in this area.

After three months on the job, I have come to at least one conclusion: it simply is not true that economists cannot agree on anything. I have been struck repeatedly by the extent to which the 50-odd economists on our staff share a common view of the "proper" role of government in protecting consumers. Such near-unanimity of opinion has greatly expedited my efforts to draft mutually acceptable position papers on pending consumer philosophical solidarity. "A more traditional view" should be construed here as the outlook of most professional economists at the FTC. That traditional view rests on two interrelated propositions.

First, economists consider the current "consumer problem" as born of excessive private and public power on several levels. For one, unwarranted market power in some of our economy's most important industries has contributed to a host of ills. When production is controlled by two or three dominant firms, the result is almost always higher than competitive prices, restricted output, lethargic management, and retarded progressiveness. While vigorous antitrust enforcement could improve the situation, political and judicial realities are such that a thorough reshaping of our economy under Section II of the Sherman Act is wishful thinking. Other methods must be found to stimulate competition.

Even massive reductions in market power would not necessarily protect consumers from the business community's disproportionate power over the

These remarks represent only the views of a member of the Federal Trade Commission staff. They are not intended to be, and should not be construed as, representative of official commission policy.

decisions of Congress, state legislatures, and the regulatory agencies. Our only salvation from this unholy alliance is sweeping campaign finance reform, establishment of a truly independent consumer protection agency willing and able to represent consumer interests during important hearings, and a dismantling of much of our current regulatory apparatus.

Finally, and perhaps most importantly, consumers are victimized by the power their own ignorance imparts to business. A wider dissemination of truly useful information on products and services would both improve consumer's chances of making intelligent purchasing decisions and, in the longer run, increase the general level of competition in our economy.

Not surprisingly, my self-styled traditional philosophy has as its second cornerstone a firm belief that the material well-being of consumers is best assured by a system of genuinely (although not perfectly) competitive markets. This is purely a pragmatic argument, not a flag-waving defense of private property, the profit motive, laissez faire, or the U.S. Chamber of Commerce. A true FTC traditionalist views public and private monopoly with equal alarm and, if pushed, might prefer socialism of some sort to capitalism without competition. Nor would massive income redistribution programs be inconsistent with a traditionalist's view of the proper economic role of government. One need not be a Marxist (Neo or otherwise) to realize that an untethered private enterprise system produces a grossly unequal distribution of wealth.

Progress, variety, and efficiency in production and distribution are, at present, best assured by competition and a reliance on market prices to communicate information. Perhaps computer technology will one day deliver us to a more promised land, but at the moment the case for socialism is a shaky one. Even assuming we could devise a socialist system capable of providing flexibility, adequate incentives, and a measure of consumer sovereignty (a feat yet to be demonstrated convincingly either on paper or in practice), we would not necessarily have tamed market power or exploitation of consumer ignorance. Efficiency considerations would compel us to retain profits as the key evaluator of business performance. If past experience in other countries is any guide, managers of government enterprises would soon realize there are easier ways to maximize profits than minimizing costs or producing quality products. If consumers were not fully informed or if the largest enterprises in an industry accounted for a substantial share of output, opportunities for collusion and product misrepresentation would remain.

While I do dismiss socialism as a dry hole, I am definitely not arguing for the status quo. A thorough overhaul of long-accepted public policies toward business is at least 30 years overdue, and we traditionalists have a few suggestions on how best to proceed. My program begins with a four-point preamble designed to capture the spirit of most economists' distaste for many of the reform proposals currently in vogue:

1. Government should not fix prices, except in those few instances where

compelling economies of scale preclude competition. We should instead first
ask why prices in an industry seem so high. If collusive pricing policies are to
blame, only a direct antitrust assault on the offending firms will reduce prices
to competitive levels. Dumping a complex regulatory apparatus on top of a
conspiracy will only produce a bigger conspiracy. If, on the other hand, the
culprit is a genuine shortage of a critical raw material or an explosion in demand,
prices should be high. Price controls will actually intensify the shortage by
discouraging expansion of productive capacity and reducing pressure on consumers to cut back on their purchases.

2. Government should not restrict choice by forcing all consumers to buy
a product or feature merely to benefit a particular industry or class of consumers. A classic example is provided by the recent Senate bill mandating AM
and FM reception capabilities for all radios sold in the United States. The Senate,
in its finite wisdom, has apparently placed the profits of FM broadcasters above
the consumer's right to buy the home or car radio that best suits his needs and
budget. The issues surrounding compulsory airbags are more complex, but it
has yet to be demonstrated that overall consumer welfare will be raised by
requiring conscientious wearers of lap and shoulder belts to pay three hundred
dollars for a device that will afford them absolutely no additional protection.

3. Government should not rely upon licensing schemes to improve the
performance of the repair service industry. Public opinion polls and analyses
of the complaint files of better business bureaus and consumer protection
agencies consistently spotlight shoddy and expensive repair work as the consumer's biggest headache. Yet the most highly touted cure—licensing of repair
establishments on the basis of employee training or diagnostic facilities—will
at best drive out a few totally inept fly-by-nighters, and runs the very real risk
of being subverted by established firms to restrict competition.[a] Moreover,
consumers would still not be able to choose intelligently among licensed shops.

4. Government should not impose elaborate conduct or disclosure rules
on business unless it is obvious that anticipated consumer benefits will far
exceed enforcement and compliance costs. Consumer protection agencies failing to heed this caveat will find themselves mired in protracted enforcement
battles that sap scarce legal and economic talent from more beneficial projects.

These admonitions supply the underpinnings for my traditionalist reform
program. If I could be economic czar for a day, I would begin by busting several
government-sanctioned cartels, an initial step that would cost virtually nothing
to implement. Specifically, I would abolish the cartel powers of the Interstate

---

[a]In a recently published study, the FTC found no difference in the incidence of fraud in
television repairs between Louisiana, which has a mandatory licensing system, and the
District of Columbia, which does not regulate TV repairs. Repair prices, however, were 20
percent higher in Louisiana. Phrean, John T., *Regulation of the Television Industry in Louisiana and California: A Case Study.* Staff Report to the Federal Trade Commission, November, 1974.

Commerce Commission, the Civil Aeronautics Board, and the Federal Maritime
Commission. I would then recommend to President Ford that he grant partial
amnesty to all government-employed price fixers and market dividers and assign
them two years alternative service at the Federal Trade Commission or the Antitrust Division of the Justice Department. Consumers should save between $3
billion and $5 billion annually, thanks to the expanded antitrust force and a
return to genuine competition in the transportation industry. In the same spirit,
I would call for the repeal of all resale price maintenance laws (known euphemistically as Fair Trade Laws) and the lifting of state-sanctioned bans on advertising the prices of eyeglasses and prescription drugs.

Lest you think I am striking a strictly nineteenth-century stance, let me
assure you that some of my recommendations will call for a hitherto unprecedented degree of governmental visibility. Television advertising in particular
cries out for a more aggressive and imaginative public policy. This is a matter
of highest priority, for recent analyses of concentration data clearly indicate
that saturation television promotions are profoundly changing this country's
industrial structure.

Until the late 1960s, economists generally believed the level of market concentration in the United States had remained relatively constant since World
War II. That is, no overall trend was evident in the market shares of the top
four or eight firms in each manufacturing industry.[b] However, researchers
recently discovered that two offsetting forces have been churning beneath this
seemingly tranquil surface. On the one hand, concentration in producer goods
industries generally has been falling. New entrants and smaller veterans have
gradually been shipping away at the dominant positions industry leaders secured
during the country's first two merger waves. Regrettably, the advent of commercial television has completely reversed this process in the broad class of consumer goods industries whose products are advertised over the air.

Data on these conflicting trends permit the closest approximation to laboratory analysis one is likely to encounter in the fuzzy world of economic research.
We can be virtually certain that the relentless concentration increases characteristic of television-oriented consumer goods industries have not been dictated
by economies of scale in production. Were this the case, a similar pattern would
surely have emerged in the heavy industrial industries. Similarly, we can dismiss
the oft-heard line that leading firms have increased their market shares simply
because they have proven themselves uniquely equipped to provide the quality
products consumers are demanding. Hard-nosed industrial buyers have apparently

---

[b]Market concentration is not to be confused with aggregate concentration, which measures the share of total manufacturing assets held by the country's largest corporations.
Aggregate concentration has increased markedly over the last 20 years as a result of
internal diversification and conglomerate mergers. This growth is not inconsistent with
stability in the level of market concentration, since companies can diversify into new
product areas without increasing their market share in any one industry.

long since learned that bigger does not necessarily mean better. As a clincher, we
now know that concentration is generally decreasing in those consumer goods
industries unable or unwilling to promote their products on television. Distilled
liquors and malt liquors provide the classic contrast. Producers of hard liquors
are prohibited from advertising on television. Between 1947 and 1970, the top
four distillers' share of the market plunged 28 percentage points. Brewing companies, on the other hand, rank among the heaviest television advertisers. Not
coincidentally, four-firm concentration in that industry increased by 25 percentage points over the same period.[c]

Evidence of a more qualitative nature can be gleaned from a brief case
history of the high fidelity industry. Almost all producers of high fidelity equipment regard television promotions as unaffordable and inappropriate. Since their
buying public tends to be relatively well informed (and, in many instances,
fanatical), effective selling appeals can be made inexpensively by placing informative ads in the various audiophile magazines. As a result, about all that is
required to break into this industry is some working capital, a bright idea, and
a one-page spread in *High Fidelity* or *Stereo Review*. Today, dozens of small-
and medium-sized firms are engaged in vigorous price and quality competition,
the fruit of which has been an almost unparalleled record of design innovations
and cost reductions. Given a less tenacious and discerning body of consumers
and an early decision by General Electric or Zenith to launch a high fidelity
component line with a series of TV blitzes, the results would have been depres-
singly predictable. The increased emphasis on costly mass-media promotion
would effectively have choked off the constant influx of new firms that has
accounted for so much of the industry's superior performance. Potential new-
comers would have been turned away in droves by the prospect of mounting
enormously costly advertising campaigns, obtaining scarce prime-time air space,
and scouring the countryside for retail dealers willing to take on an obscure
line. Meanwhile, any innovative ideas spawned within the research divisions of
entrenched industry leaders would face uncertain fates at the hands of short-
sighted, tradition-bound division managers.

I am not proposing that the FTC declare television advertising an inherently anticompetitive act (although I am eagerly awaiting the day when pay
cable TV will blunt "free" television's enormous impact on our economy).
But, at the very least, we must hit upon some method of countering the deceptions and empty claims that have contributed to the dominant market positions of big TV spenders. I fear that our current attempts to police advertising

---

[c]For a detailed analysis of the link between television advertising and market concentration, see Willard F. Mueller and Larry G. Hamm, "Trends in Industrial Market Concentration, 1947 to 1970," *Review of Economics and Statistics*, November 1974; and John
M. Blair, *Economic Concentration* (Harcourt Brace Jovanovich, Inc., 1972), pp. 321-34.
My figures for concentration changes in the brewing and distilled liquors industries are
taken from a prepublication draft of the Mueller and Hamm article.

claims with cease and desist orders and ad substantiation requirements have succeeded only in changing the nature of the deception. We can now be reasonably certain that a demonstration or factual assertion is truthful in and of itself. But we cannot be at all sure the claim has the slightest bearing on the product's utility in daily use. The alleged grease-cutting power of the detergent All is a particularly glaring case in point. It is indeed true that oil dropped into a solution of All and water will disintegrate before your eyes. It is equally true that oil dropped into any other detergent solution will just sit there. However, consumers generally do not buy a detergent for its entertainment value; and, on the basis of a controlled test in my own washing mahine, I can report to you that All enjoys no advantage whatever in removing grease from articles of clothing. Some bright young chemist at Lever Brothers no doubt stumbled across an otherwise impotent fizzing agent that could disperse oil suspended in water— and a television commercial was born.

The time is long overdue for the government to launch an advertising campaign of its own fashioned on the results of objective laboratory tests. The FTC and the Bureau of Standards should collaborate in establishing rigid test protocols for products whose performance characteristics are regularly obscured or misrepresented by advertisers. Tests could be conducted by independent laboratories under government supervision and the results used to formulate meaningful and interesting public service television and radio announcements.

This approach might not be feasible for highly complex items, such as television sets or automobiles. In such cases, attempts to quantify and assign proper weights to a galaxy of quality dimensions would no doubt produce mass confusion and distort the relative merits of competing brands. But the products in greatest need of scrutiny are the very ones most amenable to objective testing. My first candidates would be home remedies, cosmetics, bleaches, and detergents. If, for example, it is really true that all bleaches are chemically identical, and if a test of widely available brands established identical brightening capabilities as well, a simple 15-second announcement to that effect (immediately following "All in the Family") would strike a mightier blow for truth and competition in the bleach market than an avalanche of consent agreements, cease and desist orders, or ad substantiation submissions. Similarly, a short soliloquy on the true medicinal and hygienic effectiveness of mouthwashes (starring, say Mary Tyler Moore) could clear the air of conflicting and fraudulent claims overnight. Equally important, advertisers might themselves reorient their messages to stress superiorities established by the sanctioned tests, much as Honda lavished magazine copy to publicize the Civic's first place finish in the 1974 EPA mileage tests. If fortune really smiles, the testing and reporting program might stimulate price competition and rechannel research and development efforts from frills to the more substantive areas covered by the test protocols. Finally, the increased emphasis on quality and price competition would greatly enhance the ease with which new firms with better or cheaper mousetraps could break into the market.

A somewhat similar approach is needed for the repair service sector of our economy. Here the problem clearly is not extravagent advertising budgets or a lack of competitors. Consumers simply have no reliable way of gauging a repair establishment's honesty, competence, or charges until considerably after it is too late. There is probably no single cure-all for the problem, but two approaches are at least intriguing. The first of these surfaces sporadically around election or license renewal time when politicians and television stations need to don the mantel of consumer crusader in a hurry. It involves dispatching a fleet of methodically disabled Pintos or portable television sets to area repair shops and reporting the dismal results on the six o'clock news. Unfortunately, the horror stories of ineptitude, fraud, and delay usually produce nothing more tangible than a brief clamor for reform (usually in the form of a licensing program). In my view, the needed reform is simply a permanent continuation of the undercover sabotage operation. If local consumer protection agencies were to conduct monthly checks of area businesses and publish detailed results in newspapers, a double benefit would ensue. Consumers would have access to hitherto unavailable information and repairmen would never know whether the next Chevrolet to limp in the door had been deliberately doctored. Unfortunately, the plan suffers from one potentially fatal defect: timid and budget-conscious city councils might never institute it.

In that event, private polling organizations or university survey institutes might partially fill the information void. The Survey Research Center of the University of Michigan is currently developing a rather detailed telephone questionnaire designed to elicit information on Ann Arbor residents' experiences with local repair concerns. The responses will probably be very general and impressionistic; still a carefully designed and administered questionnaire might disclose significant differences in the perceived quality and honesty of service establishments.

The Michigan plan incorporates a number of features that hopefully will permit the operation to be self-financing or even profitable. The surveys will be conducted monthly to keep the information current, and thus marketable. Valuable word-of-mouth publicity will be obtained without cost by telling participants how to purchase the results during the interviews. Thought is also being given to selling the survey results over a pay channel of the Ann Arbor cable television system or from vending machines strategically located around the city. As is true of so many truly pro-competitive ideas (including the FTC's recently inaugurated Line of Business profit disclosure program), success may depend ultimately on the proponents' ability to maneuver around the multitude of legal obstructions the legal profession will inevitably place in their path.

Some of my policy recommendations may not have struck you as standard traditionalist fare, for I am certainly not advocating that the government get out and stay out of our economic lives. I am maintaining only that the consumer movement urgently needs to adopt a clear set of priorities and an allegience to policies that genuinely encourage efficiency and freedom of choice. All things considered, such sentiments may well type me as something of a revolutionary.

# Discussion

*Comment*: I would like to suggest a few structural changes we should be considering in the direction Dr. Edwards was talking about in Chapter 16. One is the concept we should be exploring, which might be called competitive public enterprise. The notion is not to have a monopolistic government agency. There is very little evidence that a government monopoly is any better than a private monopoly even in the areas discussed before. I think of strip mining, which is one of the examples of abuses just given by Professor Edwards. One of the worst strip miners in the country is the TVA, which doesn't have profits as its purpose.

On the other hand, it may be possible in some industries to have a government-created and ·financed industry either at the state or federal level, whose directors may be picked in any number of ways, not necessarily appointed by the president or the governor, which would compete and try to provide alternatives and prototypes the private system does not afford. The best illustration of the opeation of such a system is probably public television, which provides programs we could not get on private television. Probably the best illustration of this is "Sesame Street." Most people do not think of "Sesame Street" as socialistic. I could think of similar kinds of advances that might be made in other industries and in other fields if there were a government-created, competitive corporation. This was proposed in the energy field in a bill that was introduced by Senators Stevenson and Jackson and others.

A second direction might involve the election of consumer directors to corporate boards and possibly also labor union directors. I am not here thinking of publicly appointed directors but of consumer elected directors. There is a difficulty with defining who the consumers are in many fields. We have been exploring the possibilities of doing this in Los Angeles with government officials there. Our proposal is that one or two of the five directors of the Department of Water and Power (DWP) should be elected by the customers of DWP. The department is a publicly owned corporation in Los Angeles where five directors are presently appointed by the mayor. The department's customers are sent regular billing statements that could serve as a vehicle of distribution of information and as a ballot. It could work much like the current proxy statements sent to shareholders for the election of corporate directors or members of alumni boards or of other institutions.

A final suggestion for a structural change is related in a way to the concepts of criminal sanctions for corporate directors. I feel very uncomfortable with the notion of criminal sanctions. But I think some kinds of strong sanctions are needed. What I would like to propose is that shareholders should not be required to pay the costs of criminal fines or civil liability damages assessed against corporations for violations of the pollution laws or the laws protecting occupational health and safety or the marking of safe drugs. Corporation shareholders should

not pay the money for that kind of criminal conduct on the part of corporations. Cost for such abuses should be born directly by the directors. Most of
those responsible for illegal campaign contributions have now agreed voluntarily
to reimburse the corporations out of whose pockets those contributions were
made. The same thing should be done in the areas where illegal corporate conduct involves a violation of other kinds of public policy.

*Comment*: Dr. Edward's criticisms are quite legitimate insofar as they went,
but I would come back and say possibly we can "band-aid" the existing system
and keep it working fairly well. I agree that the radical economists, although
eloquently critical, are not really putting forth enough positive alternatives such
as were just proposed in Chapter 17.

Dr. Edwards warns against just importing any old kind of foregin socialism.
The only real example of full-fledged, democratic socialism I know of is the
Swedish one. In what is a very characteristic reflection of socialist thinking, the
Swedes have recently decided to centralize all governmental efforts in the
consumer policy area in a new central agency. That agency has now spent one
and one-half years trying to decide what a modern socialist policy might be
with regard to consumers. It has not come up with any kind of answers yet.
If Dr. Edwards has done some further thinking on this, I would certainly be
interested.

*Edwards*: Probably the best answer I can give is that I would like to see
a full public discussion of what socialism might mean for this country, with
the whole outpouring of ideas about different ways in which it might be
arranged. Rather than depending on old, tired models of socialism elsewhere,
let us have some fruitful productive public discussion of the different kinds
of democratically controlled institutions that might be created at all different
levels: federal, state, and local. I have no faith in any set of institutions that
I, as a radical economist sitting in my office, would design for other people.
I am hesitant to say how people ought to organize their lives. The basic thrust
of what I am saying is that we should let people decide how they want to
organize their lives by giving them some control over resources in a way they
do not have now.

There is still this pressing concern of what it is that I want. Following up
on this idea of competitive public enterprises, if the capital and productive
resources of the country were socialized, I see no reason to maintain them in
the kinds of units they have been established in now. I can imagine, for example,
all of the ideas about deregulation or deconcentration of the economy occurring
within the context of social ownership. I could envisage a series of publicly controlled institutions, of worker-controlled institutions, of community-controlled
institutions, in which the various constituent groups would participate in the
direction and control of how those enterprises were run. There are certain
problems that would have to be dealt with at the federal level or at the national
level. There are obvious disparities of income between different regions, and, as

a consequence, there would certainly be a place for some national policies about redistribution from region to region, from group to group, and so on.

In general, what I am anxious to see happen is that people who work in enterprises and people who live in communities where enterprises exist be allowed to participate in how those enterprises are run. That kind of decentralized and democratically based social enterprise is one that can take into account the kinds of problems of antisocial effects discussed in Chapter 16. Taking that as a basic premise for how one could organize things, there is likely to be a vast outpouring of ideas about how specific enterprises could be run. That is not a pie-in-the-sky idea. People today are thinking about institutional mechanisms for all sorts of things. The consumer movement is turning out ideas in great numbers of how consumers can control things and how consumers can defend their interests. We ought to have a public discussion about how this might occur in the context of social ownership.

*Comment*: Consumers need at least two things. First, they need a choice between goods, hopefully at lower prices and of good quality; and second, they need information that will give them the basis for making intelligent choices between competing goods offered to them. In terms of the first need, getting an adequate range of goods and services available, many have said what we need to accomplish this is strict enforcement of the antitrust laws to break up concentration so as to increase competition and, hopefully, produce a diversity of goods at lower prices. I hope they are wrong because it is dreaming to look to the antitrust laws for either quick or for long-term solutions. The government simply does not have the resources to enforce the antitrust laws. The FTC is bringing three major antitrust cases and the Justice Department is bringing two. That is a total of five major antitrust cases, obviously a drop in the bucket. Moreover, an antitrust case may take decades to litigate. In addition, the antitrust laws are such that it is much easier to prevent new combinations than it is to break up existing ones.

If we focus on the second element, on the other hand, we may obtain quicker results. If consumers have accurate information to make choices, they can start making intelligent consumer purchases and choose between goods that are not overpriced. One study has estimated that consumers waste approximately 50 percent of their purchasing budget by simply not knowing what they are doing. We should begin to develop institutions that would test products, rank them, and provide consumers with information through the mass media. Simply by allowing consumers to act on their own in the marketplace without governmental intervention of any other sort, we will provide an additional competitive element by enabling consumers to choose between products. I do not think that merely providing more products is the answer. I, too, have looked through the hi-fi markets and I am bewildered by the number of products available. There are hundreds of speakers, hundreds of amplifiers, hundreds of turntables.

There is no way I can rank or compare them. So merely offering me dozens does not help me make a choice. I have to have some additional information to make those choices intelligently. I would really endorse the suggestion that much can be accomplished simply by giving consumers information to make intelligent choices.

# 18

Current Corporate Programs
Responding to
Consumer Problems

*Raymond A. Bauer* and
*David B. Kiser*

Part I of this chapter describes our overall program on the implementation of "social" policies in business organizations, and part II, by David Kiser, discusses what we have learned about the implementation of consumerism programs specially.

## Part I

About three years ago, Professor Dick Walton, the director of our Division of Research at the Graduate School of Business Administration, Harvard University suggested that the area generally called "business social responsibility" was notably lacking in empirical content. Realizing it is easy to make a splash in an empty bucket, a number of us moved to correct that situation. We have now published a couple of books *(The Corporate Social Audit* and *Corporate Social Accounting)*, a half dozen scholarly articles, written a couple of dozen teaching cases, finished several theses, and have two books and several monographs in progress. Our work has been supported by Harvard, several private foundations, and the National Science Foundation. Our present effort involves about a half dozen members of the faculty, two full-time research assistants, and several doctoral students. Part of our work has been concerned with the measurement of corporate social performance.

Early in 1972, Robert Ackerman called attention to the fact that little or nothing was known about the management problems of implementing social policies. The literature up to that time was deficient in three related respects. It either explicitly or implicitly treated the motivation of top management as the crucial, and perhaps the only important, variable in the responsiveness of corporations. It failed to reflect the extent to which "social" issues were interwoven with regular business operations. It drew a distinction between "optional" and "mandatory" issues in a manner that paralleled the aforementioned emphasis on the motivation of top management. It was as if either top management were convinced or a law were passed the matter would be neither interesting nor difficult.

Recognizing that most of the major new issues confronting corporations— pollution control, equal employment, health and safety, consumerism, community relations, and the like—required changes in behavior at the operating level of business organizations, Ackerman could see the will of the chief executive

officer could not by itself insure the desired changes in behavior. His own prior
work and that of others indicated that implementation would pose special problems in the complex product and market divisionalized structures that pre-
dominate among our largest firms. He was able to identify a number of dilemmas that flowed from the structure, operating styles, and systems of reward
and control of such organizations. Briefly, the structures were designed to afford
substantial autonomy to operating divisions that were often several levels below
top management. The control system was designed to measure the financial
performance of the operating units, and the heads of operating units were
rewarded on that basis.

Ackerman's early intensive work in two major organizations suggested a
model of the implementation process that subsequent resesearch has only rein-
forced and elaborated. The basics of this model were communicated in an article: "How Companies Respond to Social Demands" in the *Harvard Business
Review.*[1]

The essence of his model is a sequence of stages. The first stage is that at
which the chief executive officer becomes committed on an issue and makes
statements to that effect. Operating executives wonder how seriously they
should take this new potential demand on their time, attention, and financial
resources. Nothing happens.

In the second stage, a staff specialist is appointed who, for the first time,
makes a detailed analysis of the problem and of the resources required to implement general policy to which the chief executive wishes to commit the organization. The staff specialist tries to get compliance by exhortation and persuas-
ion, but little happens. However, the staff specialist is likely to make some form
of "audit" of performance, which forms the precursor of an information system
and a more formal policy statement is required because existing statements are
too vague to be guides to action.

All of the above activities, however, are prefatory to successful implementation, which does not really begin until the operating units accept responsibility.
This "stage three" may come about with varying degrees of orderliness. Frequently it occurs as a result of some trauma—a lawsuit, bad publicity—that
causes top management to express its serious intent in an unequivocal fashion.
Sometimes it occurs as a result of deliberate, orderly administrative steps.

However it comes about, the features of stage three are a regular information system that lets mangement track the performance of operating units,
a review of existing procedures and the establishment of administrative arrangements consistent with the intent of policy, training of personnel where relevant, and ultimately a revision of the reward system whereby executives are
evaluated.

A little reflection brings one to the realization that if this procedure were
followed for many issues over a long period, a firm could be encumbered with
a very complex control system indeed. This led us to the speculation that full

institutionalization of policy occurs when compliance becomes so automatic that there is no necessity to pay it further attention. A student paper tracing the history of the relationship of U.S. Steel to the steelworkers union confirmed every one of Ackerman's stages in specific detail, and also our final speculation. After a number of years, the new pattern of labor relations became so habitual that the control and reward system that U.S. Steel had constructed simply withered away.[2]

The broad outline of the implementation process has furnished a conceptual core around which a coherent research agenda has evolved.

Ackerman spent much of 1973–74 completing his book *Managing Corporate Responsibility*, which elaborates the model of the implementation process, building not only on Ackerman's own field research, but on the research of others associated with the program.[3] This descriptive account is accompanied by practical suggestions for more effective implementation. Ackerman established soundly one of his main theses, namely, that corporate responsiveness is inextricably part of the regular operations of the firm. His rich clinical detail gives one a sense of the difficulty and complexity of the learning process involved.

Alden Lank, building on Ackerman's work, concentrated in detail on the role of corporate staff in the implementation of a series of social programs in two large diversified firms.[a] This thesis gives a more elaborate view of the organizational problems of implementation at "stage two." Various of our case studies have been aimed at illuminating a number of aspects of the implementation process. In the light of Ackerman's stage model of implementation, the issue of social measurement took on new perspectives.

Ranne Warner has done an intensive study of affirmative action in a large public university, focusing on the development of an employee information system.[2] The information system is looked at on the one hand from the point of view of its role in implementation, and on the other hand from the point of view of the organizational and administrative problems of developing such a system. (This case has not yet been released.)

In two other (as yet unreleased) cases, Fred Foulkes and Louis Rocquet studied a system for auditing OSHA compliance, and Rikk Larsen studied what appears to be a very advanced "stage three" administrative system for affirmative action in separate divisions of the same large firm.[c]

Again, building on Ackerman's work, Murray has finished a thesis, *The Implementation of Social Policies in Commercial Banks,* based on interviews and observations in seven banks, two of which he studied intensively. One of the original reasons for selecting banks as organizations to study had been the fact that their internal structure is simpler than that of the type of firms.

[a]Lank's field research was supported by funds from NSF.

[b]Warner's work is supported by the Rockefeller Brothers Fund.

[c]The field work of Foulkes, Rocquet, and Larsen as well as that of Murray was supported jointly by funds from NSF and the Division of Research.

with which we had gained our earlier experience. Since a bank is in basically
one line of business understood by top management, it is not unusual for top
management to intervene directly in operations without having to cajole the
cooperation of middle-level managers. Our anticipation was that the process
of implementation would be smoother and more rapid. This anticipation
was by and large wrong. The process was different but nevertheless quite protracted. Relatively complex issues required changes in regular operating behavior. For example, it took approximately eight years for each of the two
banks to develop the administrative arrangements for an effective program
of lending to minority businesses.

The way in which the implementation process differed in banks, however, was instructive. Because top management could intervene in operations
it had the opportunity to learn by doing. This highlighted a distinction between "technical learning" and "administrative learning" that had been latent
but not explicit in our thinking to that point. It is quite a different thing for
a single officer of the bank to learn the technical job of lending to a new type
of clientele and for the bank to learn what management steps are required in
order to get that particular job done on a bank-wide basis.

In effect, this distinction between technical and administrative learning
not only was a conceptual contribution, but served to define the mission of
our research more sharply. Clearly our main misson is concerned with administrative (or managerial) learning. It is not to become specialists in the substance of all or any of the issues with which corporations are involved, but
in the administrative, managerial, and organizational matters that enable
the corporation to deal with those issues.

We have learned a great deal in the past three years. The most general
lesson we have learned is that the implementation of social policies is indeed
a long complex process of organizational learning that requires a considerable
amount of structural change in the organization. In turn, our own most
general hope is that by delineating the stages and steps of this process we
will enable organizations to pass through them more rapidly. Most still have
a long way to go. We also hope to contribute to a more general understanding
of the problems of implementation of *any* new policy, whether it be strictly
"social" or not. From the point of view of the social critic or the public
administrator responsible for the implementation of specific laws or regulations, we hope to give him or her a better comprehension of what she or he
is asking the organization to do, and thereby a better basis for evaluating
whether or not a good faith effort is being made.

We have received repeated reactions of incredulity from audiences such
as this when we have suggested that four, five, or six years might be the
irreducible minimum period for institutionalizing a social policy in a complex
organization. This "delay" is invariably interpreted as lack of good intent
at the top of management. But, the necessary sequence of steps indicates

that there is a limit to the extent to which time can be compressed. (Dave
Kiser, in part II, has selected for illustration a problem that on the surface
seems to be preposterously simple, but which took a couple of years to handle.
Try to figure out how you would expedite implementation.)

A second general lesson we have learned is the distinction between technical and administrative learning. There is a vast difference between learning
how to do something, and learning how to get something done. Most organizations are unaware of the need for administrative learning until they have
experienced a conspicuous failure in their efforts to implementation.

A final general lesson has been to understand more explicitly the relationship between what are usually called "social" issues and the regulat conduct
of business. There are several specifiable ways in which the two are inseparable.

First, it is not clear whether some issues are "social" or "business." Consumerism, of course, is a prime example. But, what about community relations? Specifically, what about an insurance agent working on a community
project? Or a utility, which is dependent on community good will for rate
increases?

Second, most "social" issues have to be implemented via regular business
operations. Equal employment opportunity depends on the behavior of everyone in the organization down to the lowest line manager. Pollution control
involves engineering and production. Except for complaint handling (which
is sometimes surprisingly isolated from the rest of the organization), every
consumer issue involves marketing, or advertising, or quality control, or
production, or product design, or some combination of these.

Next, the pursuance of any social issue competes for scarce resources
with traditional business activities. It is customary to think of money as the
scarce resource. In some instances money is the main resource on which social
issues place demands. Capital investments in pollution control are the most
obvious. However, more often the scarce resources are the time, attention,
and energy of top executives.

Once more, the pursuance of social issues may improve regular business
practices. In one instance, the organization of community relations teams
opened up communications across functions where they had not existed. Or
a "social" issue such as free checking for the elderly may lead a bank to the
discovery of a new profitable service. Most often it causes a reexamination of
regular business activities with the frequent revelation that they are in need
of improvement apart from the social issue which prompted the examination.
Tackling pollution control often brings about improved design of industrial
processes. More usual, however, is the discovery that a firm's personnel function is quite thoroughly fouled up. This discovery is a result of trying to
implement an affirmative actions plan, and has repercussions way beyond the
issue of affirmative action. As a result, many a personnel department is in
the process of being thoroughly overhauled.

For this reason we have abandoned the term "social responsibility" and substituted the term "corporate responsiveness." What we believe we are studying is the development of a corporate capacity to identify, sort out, and implement new issues. It is true that many or most of the new issues with which the corporation is presently dealing stem from recently expanded demands on business's social performance. But the management problems are management problems, not social problems. By no means do I mean to be fatuous about what is being achieved, nor am I necessarily very confident about what will emerge. What I would contend is that in referring to the development of a responsive corporation we are specifying the name of the game being played, but not predicting if the game will be played successfully—although I have hopes.

### Part II

We do believe that monitoring corporate responses to consumerism serves as a leading indicator, if you will, of how corporations manage social issues. Why consumerism? For one thing, consumerism seeks to modify the way corporations design and market their products. Although pollution control might affect plant design and location, and minority hiring issues might affect personnel policies, consumerism issues such as product safety, truth in advertising, and product quality impact on the very bread and butter of the corporation—on the marketing of its products. To the extent such demands add to the unit costs of such products, profit margins are jeopardized and management attention is increased. But more than that, discretion over product design and marketing has, until lately, been left entirely in the hands of the private producer, and it is this power that is being eroded rather than profit. Both demands suggest some organizational response on the part of the corporation.

Second, we do the businessman and the consumer advocate a disservice if we project the image of consumerism as housewife vs. corporation, or even government agency vs. corporation. It is unquestionably a social movement aimed at tipping the balance of buyers' and sellers' rights more in favor of the buyer. But a social movement by whom? Some of the most elaborate consumer programs in product safety and product quality have emerged from producer vs. producer: many small producers vs. a large producer, many large producers vs. many small producers, and so on. The classic example is the meat packing industry, where large producers sought federal quality standards to prevent price cutting by smaller producers, and achieved them. So consumerism is an economic shuffle that can push demands from all sectors of our society onto the large corporation. How a response to those demands is fashioned by the corporation can hopefully give us insight into other corporate social issues as well.

I want to offer you some observations on how large corporations manage consumer issues. I draw my observations from extensive field studies over the past year in four large consumer-goods corporations. I do not offer them as truths, but simply as propositions that may be helpful in describing the policy system all of us—educators, businessmen, and activists—must interact with.

They are not typical observations. The conventional wisdom found in the literature is inevitably of the "how-to" variety: for the consumer affairs manager, how to organize the consumer complaint department, how to handle toll-free complaint phone lines, how to deal with government agencies and consumer activists, and even how to get the president's attention more often. The activist, in turn, can learn about organizing consumer boycotts, lobbying, getting proposals onto corporate proxies, and the like. Neither gets at the heart of the matter. For consumer demands, quite simply, compete for corporate resources along with demands for research, advertising, plant and equipment, cost-cutting improvements, and every other activity that goes into running a large corporation. The real question to be answered is this: How do individual managers decide to commit themselves—their time, their budgets, and possibly their careers—in support of consumer projects that necessarily take away time and funds from more conventional business concerns?

Let me introduce you to the problem with an example that concerns an effort undertaken by a large grocery-products manufacturer to facilitate its product safety recall procedure. In 1972 the chairman of the company, which I will call IEP Corporation, expanded the job of the director of quality control to include food safety. At the time, the Consumer Product Safety Act was nearing passage, and the chairman wanted someone to have the direct responsibility for implementing the provisions of the act. One such provision called for notifying the commission within a brief period if it became known that a hazardous product had reached the marketplace, and along with the notification including plans for recalling the hazardous product if that should be deemed necessary.

The director of quality control at IGP appointed his immediate subordinate to the post of corporate director of product safety and asked him to prepare a product safety recall procedure. The procedure would identify what needed to be done in case of a recall in order to comply with IGP's own high standards as well as the law itself. The task was completed during the summer of 1972. Among other things, the procedure called for each case of product to be legibly coded with information pertaining to its manufacture: the plant in which it was produced, the month, day, year, and the shift of operation. Thus in the event of a recall, cases suspected of contamination or whatever could be easily identified no matter where they were located in the company's distribution system. In addition, records were to be kept showing the number of total cases packed under each date code and the number of cases shipped, by date code by destination. It was quite straightforward, and the new policy was sent out to all segments of the manufacturing and marketing divisions.

The new policy, however, was not one to cause a great deal of attention by the operating managers—those who were responsible for selling specified amounts of product at specified cost. IGP had a strong safety record, and millions were spent every year on maintaining exacting standards of quality control and plant hygiene. When problems did occur, they were usually due to bad ingredients provided by IGP's suppliers, and those ingredients were carefully checked whenever they entered an IGP plant. What's more, the policy seemed normative rather than declarative in tone, pointing out what *should* be done in the event of a recall, not what *would* be done. In response, not much *got* done.

During the ensuing 18 months, product recalls by other organizations were much in the news. Bon Vivant had been forced to close its doors due to a disastrous recall of vichyssoise soup infected with botulism. Campbell Soups spent millions on a large recall of product suspected of contamination. IGP itself had some minor recalls involving salmonella contamination but in each instance the suspected cases had not moved far enough through the distribution system to present headaches. Nonetheless, the director of product safety wondered if IGP could handle a major recall. Meanwhile, in the Manufacturing Division of IGP, some date-coding equipment was already in use in each of IGP's plants. Plant site, month, day, year, and shift were supposedly stamped on every shipping case as it moved on conveyors toward warehouses or trucks. However, 80 percent of the stamped codes were illegible even at a close distance. Ink pads would run dry without being noticed; different case sizes run on the same packing lines would render some equipment ineffective; too much ink would smear the codes as the packs went by at high speed; and so on. This state of affairs prompted complaints from distributors in the field, because they found it hard to rotate their physical inventory accurately on a first-in, first-out basis. Their complaints had been received understandingly by various managers in the manufacturing division, but the funds necessary for upgrading the date-coding equipment had never been approved by the Manufacturing Division's vice-president. They simply were needed elsewhere for cost cutting, new capacity, and other new equipment. The fact that the corporate director of product safety now wanted the date codes more legible did not change a thing. The distributors would simply have to do the best they could.

In the summer of 1973, one year after his initial overture, the director of product safety went a step further. Under the signature of the executive vice-president of all the operating groups, a new set of elaborate product recall procedures was issued to all the plants and distribution centers. The new policy called explicitly for date-coding records to be kept for three years on certain products that were "bacteriologically sensitive" or more prone to contamination over time. The Quality Control Department would be responsible for keeping the records for that period. No explicit reference was made, however, to improving the legibility of the date codes themselves. That was in the summer of 1973.

During the next nine months, a curious thing happened. A packaging engineer in the Manufacturing Division, who had responsibility for the technical operation of the packing lines, took it upon himself to have a study done of alternative means of improving the legibility of the case coding. You see, it was on his shoulders that the complaints from the distribution centers were falling, and he wanted to be prepared should someone ask him to look into the problem. The study called for $100,000 to be spent immediately for date-coding equipment. At the time of the initial study, legibility had been very poor, around 20 percent. After the study, however, legibility improved to around 50 percent in a Hawthorne-like reaction by the plant workers to the attention paid them by corporate executives running around the plants checking date codes. More time was being spent to insure that the dating stamps were in good condition, well-inked, and changed as often as necessary.

In April of 1974, the group director of quality control decided independently of the packaging engineer to appoint a task force to insure the effectiveness of IGP's recall procedures. Immediately, this task force realized that without legible case codes, no accurate records could be kept, and certainly no accurate recall could be administered if the need arose. So, the task force went to the Manufacturing Division's packaging engineer and asked him if a study could be done showing the problems with case coding and the alternative solutions that might be undertaken to improve legibility. The packaging engineer, of course, gave them the study he had done in response to the distributors complaints and was quite pleased with himself for his foresight.

It was at this point in time, in late spring of this year, that things really started getting hairy. To begin with, the Division's quality control director drew up a capital request for $100,000 worth of date-coding equipment and fired it off to the Manufacturing Division's vice-president for approval. The latter could easily have approved it if he wanted, for he could spend up to $125,000 by himself without going for higher approval. But he stalled on it. You see, he had always had a pet dream of doing all the printing on shipping cases in-plant, rather than farming it out to contractors. By doing so, not only would he recover some unit costs, but he would free up quite a bit of plant floor space, which was now chock-full of ready-to-pack cartons. So he instigated a new study to check into the capital costs of silk-screening all case printing in each plant, and combining the request for the date-coding equipment within the larger request for printing equipment.

At this point in time, it should be understood that the manufacturing vice-president knew that some expenditure of funds for upgrading the case-coding equipment was inevitable. However, he knew that if he could combine his desires with those of quality control, he had a much better chance of getting both projects completed. His hopes dimmed, however, with two other events during the summer. First, his request for a cost estimate for in-plant printing came back with a whopping price tag of $600,000 for capital and higher operating costs than could be purchased from outside contractors. There went that idea. Second, because of the tight money situation, his project approval limit was cut from $125,000 to $25,000. Now, even if he wanted to approve the simpler proposal, he would have to seek group executive approval. Furthermore, because the simpler proposal added to his direct costs rather than reducing them, he would probably have to seek budget relief as well, as prospect he did not at all relish.

Finally, in August of 1974, this researcher personally investigated the quality of date-coding in one of IGP's plants. With no capital improvements, reports showed that legibility was running at 85 to 95 percent of all cases packed and had been for some time. Interviews with quality control people confirmed these figures as accurate. While such a percentage was not good enough to insure 100 percent recovery of product in a serious recall, it was much better than the figures reported for that plant. What had happened? For one thing, there had been some improvement in the figures since the 1973 policy statement. Twenty percent legibility simply was not good enough to support the record keeping the policy demanded. Thus, keeping the coding machines operating properly had risen in priority, and legibility had improved.

This improvement notwithstanding, the legibility figures reported in the study requested by the packaging engineer had to be understated. What's more, the group director of quality control had not revised the figures in the capital request—and well he could have since the plant records were sent directly to him for summary and safekeeping. One might conclude that the legibility statistics were understated to strengthen the case for capital improvements, and that the pressure to do so came both from distribution and quality control. It came from distribution in order to get distributor complaints down, and from quality control to insure the nervous corporate directors of quality control and product safety that IGP was, in fact, prepared to undertake a major product recall. At the conclusion of my field work, events were moving slowly toward approval of the $100,000 date-coding package, in spite of the manufacturing vice-president's reluctance.

The case serves to illustrate how complex these things can be, and how personal stakes and careers can get in the way of a project regardless of how individual managers might view the merits of the project itself. The project essentially went through three phases. First, it was *initiated* by corporate staff members who were concerned with IGP's ability to handle a major product recall. Second, it received *impetus* from distribution and division quality control who saw the potential gains from the project and prepared an overstated case in support of it. It also received impetus from the cut in approval limits, for then the manufacturing vice-president knew that the sponsors could go right to the top with it if he refused to go alone. So he attempted to combine the project with one of his own, but was unable to justify the expense. He then had to go along. At last, the project moved toward final approval with a strong coalition of corporate and distribution people leading the way. One could now say that IGP had complied with the intent of the Consumer Product Safety Act, some two years after its passage.

Large companies seem to respond initially to a new consumer demand in much the same way that they have responded to other social issues in the past. By virtue of differences in the structure of the firm, the formula that tends to emerge is that they appoint a specialist, as IGP did, or they form a corporate committee, or they simply delegate the handling of the demand to an operating division. It may be desirable to avoid this kind of gut reaction, as you will see in a moment. At any rate, the undertaking of any of these approaches signals the beginning of the corporate response process. Shortly thereafter, as the specialist, division, or committee begins to grapple with the issue, technical learning begins. It is characterized by a growing proficiency in analyzing, diagnosing, and answering social demands and by a better understanding of what the flap is all about.

Much later in time, say, from one to three years, administrative learning begins. Here is where upper management begins to learn how to organize to manage social programs more efficiently. In the case of IGP, administrative learning is evidenced by two events: First, the rephrasing of the corporate recall policy by the corporate product safety director suggests the beginning of an appreciation of the dividing line between action suggested by a policy and the action itself. A simple normative statement of a desired policy was seen not to be enough to inspire compliance. Second, the construction of the separate task force by the Division's quality control director to overhaul the product recall machinery implies the beginning of a system to handle product recalls routinely. When a system has been established to handle social demands we can accept the event as a clear measure of administrative learning. Finally, the time comes when resources must be committed to a project of any significance. The pace and quality of the allocation of resources for consumer projects depends to a great extent on which one of our three organizational units—specialists, corporate committees, or divisions—initiates the project. More specifically:

1.  If a top corporate committee initiates the project, the division manager whose budget is affected will view the project as having high legitimacy. He will tend to estimate the costs of the project as very high in order to protect his budget, but will try to complete the project for a much lower amount.

2.  If a group of specialists initiates the same project, as in the case of IGP, the division manager will view the project as having very low legitimacy. The specialists will tend to estimate the costs of project on the low side, in order to facilitate getting the division manager's approval. But the actual project costs will be relatively high, due to the increased time required for jockeying and budget approval.

3.  Finally, if the project is initiated by the division manager as a routine
    management matter, he will obviously view it with very high legitimacy.
    He will estimate the lowest possible costs since only he loses from inflating
    those estimates, and he will complete the project at the lowest cost of the
    three alternatives, all other things being equal.

**Notes**

1. Robert Ackerman, "How Companies Respond to Social Demands,"
*Harvard Business Review*, July-August 1973.

2. George R. Houget, "United States Steel and the Acceptance of Union-
ism: Some Implications for Contemporary Management," a student paper, Harvard Business School, April 21, 1973.

3. Robert Ackerman, *Social Challenge to Business* (Cambridge: Harvard
University Press, 1975).

# Discussion

*Comment:* I am concerned about the real time-frame needs of companies when responding to externally imposed regulation.

*Bauer:* We are a fickle society in any substantial sense as far as the broad events taking place are concerned. About the middle of the 1960s there was a de facto decision made in the industrialized world to impose new standards of performance in our institutions. Part of this was a revolt against the GNP as the sole standard. I will give you two pieces of evidence of why I put that data there. One is a positive piece of evidence. We had a book in press called *Social Indicators* in 1965. My aspirations for that book were very very modest. I thought it might irritate some people who in turn might do the job right. Suddenly it went off like gang-busters, we gave away hundreds of copies before we could publish it. The social indicators movement is now worldwide.

The British have had a publication out now for three years, the Germans have one out, the French have one out, the Israelis have been doing something like that, the Swiss have one out, and we even have one out. The negative thing to put the dating on there is that if you go back to public opinion data and see when the estimation of the performance of our institutions started to turn, it was in 1965-66. It is right straight across the board. It was just this period.

What we are dealing with essentially is the basic social decisions of the broadest nature. You can find people who are backing off a little on pollution control, etc., but we are really dealing with something that is broad and profound. In the mid-sixties, industrialized societies made a mammoth decision to measure the performance of the society strictly in economic terms. You can see this creeping in place after place after place. But that notion has really taken over and it is ambiguous. It is really very symptomatic of the broad resolution that we don't measure progress anymore by technical and economic terms.

*Question:* What is the difference in implementation of a product innovation and a social change?

*Bauer:* A product innovation presents somewhat different problems. I have partial answers to your question. The basic problem is if in a complex organization you want to push a policy down from above, and get it into the operation of the organization is there any difference between the way you would do that than with health and safety, or equal employment, versus corporate purchasing policy? Or a corporate-wide way of handling electronic data processing systems? It turns out there isn't any of the others for us to look at yet, but the preliminary look we have had of the electronic data processing system certainly suggests some broad similarities. The most uniform thing is the fact that when something like this starts out no one knows what they have to learn. That's a funny thing to have to say, but that, too, characterizes the whole stream of events. Because once you get a road map such as that for the electronic data processing system, you can say you move from stage to stage: her are the administrative problems you are going to be confronted with, and here are the sort of responses available for you to make. This is the next stage you will go through.

I think you can do well with equal employment, and maybe some of the others, but the final list just hasn't been circulated. Somehow, most companies, in spite of the existence of such a map, will put their head down and go plan their own anyway. There is some learning across companies that is taking place, and we are going to see more of it, but that is the main thing. I suspect we are going to find some real similarities and that the similarities may be very general, but they also may be very specific to the company.

# 19

**Epilogue**

*Mary Gardiner Jones* and
*David M. Gardner*

A premise clearly accepted by conference participants is that consumer concerns about the performance of the marketplace must be dealt with. There is general agreement that interaction among consumers and businessmen as well as government representatives is important and must continue. As some have said: "We agree that we are all in this thing together." Hope has been expressed that business-consumer interaction can be accomplished by a genuine cooperative effort to share mutual problems and negotiate differences. It is agreed that neither consumer nor business is a monolithic entity and that its spokesperson must not be so regarded. The process is seen by some as evolutionary and the need for rational discourse without the use of the half-truth and inuendo as essential.

This book provides hard evidence that while the donkey's attention has been gained, there are still significant gaps in perception as to where the real problems lie. The dichotomy between the role consumers can and should play and their power to affect change is still in sharp dispute. The business perspective stresses the costs of government regulation and its impact on their competitive position. Consumers stress the deficiencies in the play of market forces to furnish them with the information they need; the quality of product they deserve; and the protection from the environmental impacts of manufacturing processes they believe necessary. Similarly, business representatives tend to rely more strongly on marketplace forces as the dynamic ones for responsiveness to consumer concerns while consumer spokespersons stress the need in many areas for other modes of intervention in order to insure needed change. Consumers see the individual consumer's refusal to buy as an inherently ineffective marketplace change agent and look to other strategies such as group boycotts or direct input of consumer views into the decision-making process as necessary to make consumer sovereignty a more meaningful concept. The issue has also been posed but not answered as to whether in the long-run consumer issues could in fact be solved by cooperation or whether the desired interaction must be by the adversary process and in confrontation format or by more systemic structural changes in the economic system.

Concerns have been voiced in this connection as to who can really speak for "the" consumer, whether individual consumers do not in fact hold widely differing views as to what is in their best interest, and who really is the consumer anyway? Questions have been raised as to whether consumers are intelligent, knowledgeable, and sophisticated or helpless, gullible, and naive.

Clearly, neither business nor consumer groups are monolithic. Merely

because one consumer talks about an abusive business practice does not necessarily constitute an attack on all business and merely because one consumer calls
for socialism, it does not follow that all consumer groups believe in that.

Do consumers have any greater insights than management into the solution of problems? Will not socialization of management decisions encounter
these same problems regardless of who is making the decision? Doubt has
been expressed with the assumption that the imposition of social controls on
management will necessarily impose social responsibility on management. An
alternative method is seen as impressing management—through education and
other means—with the need to consider social goals along with profit in its
decision-making responsibilities.

The major consumer problems have been identified as follows:

1. *Product diversity problems:* Is the marketplace producing optimum
product options in terms of product quality, durability, and price. In this
same area, product quality problems must also be looked at more broadly
in terms of worker dissatisfaction and the growing concern of all citizens for
quality of life goals along with their material needs.

2. *Consumer information problems:* How do consumers know what
they are buying? How do they get reliable information, referred to by someone as "society's underinvestment in consumer information"? This issue has
provoked more discussion and comment than many others. The areas for which
information is regarded as essential embrace not only such things as product
quality and reliability, market-basket price programs, and data on specific ind-
dustries such as insurance, but also such broad areas as the needs for deconsump-
tion in our economy today, the impact of political and judicial institutional
decisions on consumer issues, the quality of governmental performance, and the
existence of innovative governmental consumer programs. The problem of information delivery systems, particuarly to the elderly and low-income groups,
has been referred to and the point stressed that industry has a critical role to
play in disseminating product information along with the need for expanded
consumer education programs.

3. *Consumer redress mechanisms:* Consumers' needs for systematic ways
to present their grievances and compel a hearing on them have been stressed,
as well as the view that industry should respond to these needs and create such
redress mechanisms.

4. *Marketplace transaction problems:* Credit and warranties have been
singled out as creating the most serious problems for the consumer.

5. *Product externality issues:* The impact of product use on third persons
(noncustomers) or on the environment has been stressed as an area of important
concern to consumers.

Concerning the role of government in solving consumer problems in the
marketplace, searching questions have been raised as to whether government
programs really respond to consumer needs and if the government reflects the

concerns of all consumers. The importance of examining the cost of regulation and its impact on competition—worldwide as well as domestic—is essential.

The general subject of the direction in which solutions to the various consumer problems can be considered gives rise to a wide variety of opinions. Some stress the importance of consumer education as an essential element in the development of solutions to marketplace deficiencies. Some see this essentially as a responsibility of the school system.

Government is seen as playing a potentially significant role in product testing and standards development and also in the area of information dissemination to the public, not only with respect to the results of governmental product-testing programs but also about particular industry data, food prices, the role of consumer affairs offices, and the activities of corporations. Information dissemination is also seen as a responsibility of industry and as a potential function of a national nonprofit institute. Such an institute is seen as performing a vital service in compiling reliable data on existing consumer protection legislation and regulations in effect throughout the 50 states, in evaluating the effectivenss of such regulatory programs, in developing cost-benefit data on alternative solutions to consumer problems, and establishing a priority of consumer concerns through market surveys and other techniques. The competitive system is also seen as one of continuing vitality and as an essential force to meet many of the consumer's marketplace problems, particularly those dealing with product reliability, quality, and price.

Consumer and business representatives tend to differ in their perception of the continuing role of the consumer movement with many consumers pessimistic and the business participants optimistic about its continuing effectiveness as a change agent. Business underscores the inherent slowness of the process of developing ideas and translating them into action programs but expresses the belief that the idea-generating stage had been passed and that business is now beginning to phase into its activities many of the ideas and issues discussed in this book.

There is still must work to be done to bring consumer and business perceptions of the marketplace and of consumer needs and concerns into closer phase. This book makes clear that meaningful accomplishments have been made, but that much remains yet to be done. Business is clearly very much aware of consumers in a way it never has been before. Partly this is the result of the limited action of government bodies, and partly the result of pressures from consumer groups. But, as this book points out, there is no longer a ready acceptance of government as a solution to restoring equilibrium. We are now just beginning to be aware that solutions, especially government solutions, impose certain costs. However, again, too little hard work has been put into developing the trade-offs that must be made. But the nature of these trade-offs is not well understood and, unfortunately, no meaningful attempts have been made to cope with this basic issue of how consensus and trade-offs can be developed.

Although it is clear that some steps of increasing information available to consumers have been made and more are on the way, it is not clear which and to what extent marketplace problems can or even should be addressed by information dissemination alone. This area requires much more systematic attention than it has received to date.

Furthermore, as pointed out repeatedly in this book, we have yet to discover how consumer inputs into the decision process of firms can be accomplished in a way in which influence will be both useful and meaningful. The consumer must be sovereign, but the means and the extent of this sovereignty are still not resolved.

# List of Off-campus Participants

Ms. Aileen Adams
School of Law
University of California
405 Highland Avenue
Los Angeles, CA   90024

Mr. Charles F. Allison
Group Vice President
Booz, Allen and Hamilton, Inc.
135 South LaSalle Street
Chicago, IL   60602

Mr. Peter Barash
Office of Congressman Rosenthal
House of Representatives
2453 Rayburn Building
U.S. Congress
Washington, D.C.   20515

Mr. Stanley J. Boulier
Assistant Vice-President
American Telephone and Telegraph
    Company
195 Broadway
New York, NY   10007

Mr. Joseph Bres
Exxon Corporation
P.O. Box 77001
Houston, TX   77001

Ms. Peggy Charren
President
Action for Children's Television
46 Austin Street
Newtonville, MA   02160

Ms. Sherry Chenoweth
Minnesota Office of Consumer Affairs
5th Floor, Metro Square Building
St. Paul, MN   55101

Mr. Grant Clark
Vice-President of Executive & Profes-
    sional Banking Division
Northern Trust Company
50 South LaSalle Street
Chicago, IL   60690

Professor Geoffrey Cowan
School of Law
University of California
405 Highland Avenue
Los Angeles, CA   90024

Mr. Bill Davis
Vice-President
Sherwin Williams
101 Prospect Avenue, N.W.
Cleveland, OH   44115

Mr. Ethan I. Davis
Vice-President
Policyowner Service & Public Affairs
    Department
Prudential Insurance Company
Corporate Headquarters
Newark, N.J.   07101

Mr. Frank J. Dawson
Director of Market Services
People Gas Company
122 South Michigan Avenue
Chicago, IL   60603

Ms. Esther Dyson
Council on Economic Priorities
84 Fifth Avenue
New York, NY   10011

Mr. James Fox
Director of Consumer Relations
Goodyear Company
1144 East Market
Akron, OH   44316

171

**Ms. Margaret A. Freeston**
Special Assistant to the General
    Counsel
Consumer Product Safety Commission
Washington, D.C.   20207

**Ms. Barbara Gilhaus**
ABL Community Unit School
    District, #6
Broadlands, IL   61816

**Mr. James Goodwin**
The President's Office
University of California
Berkeley, CA   94720

**Mr. M.J. Henrichs**
Corporate Vice-President & President
Pharmaceutical Products Division
Abbott Laboratories
Abbott Park
North Chicago, IL   60064

**Mr. Carl E. Horn**
Assistant Vice-President
Planning and Rate Administration
Illinois Bell Telephone Company
225 West Randolph
Chicago, IL   60606

**Mr. John A. Howard**
Professor of Marketing
Graduate School of Business
Columbia University in the City of
    New York
New York, NY   10027

**Ms. Susan Irion**
Eisner Food Stores
Director of Consumer Affairs
Division of Jewel Companies
Champaign, IL   61820

**Mr. Leonard A. Jasper**
Down Chemical Company
P.O. Box 68511
Indianapolis, IN   46268

**Ms. Jiffy Johnson**
Sanjamon State University
Springfield, IL   62701

**Mr. Richard Jorgensen**
First National Bank
30 Main Street
Champaign, IL   61820

**Mr. J.A. Kosh**
Director of Corporate Test Center
AMF Incorporated Corporate Test
    Center
695 Hope Street
Stamford, Ct   06907

**Professor Philip Kotler**
Graduate School of Management
Northwestern University
Evanston, IL   60201

**Mr. Victor H. Kramer**
Center for Public Representation
520 University Avenue
Madison, WI   53703

**Mr. Jerry Lamet, Esq.**
Federal Trade Commission
55 East Monroe Street
Chicago, IL   60603

**Ms. Susan Lauer**
Consumer Coordinator
General Electric Company
5600 West 73rd Street
Chicago, IL   60638

**Dr. Fabian Linden**
Director
Consumer Research Division
The Conference Board
845 Third Avenue
New York, NY 10022

**Ms. Bonnie Martin**
Manager
Consumer Communications & Special
   Events
General Mills, Inc.
9200 Wayzata Boulevard
Minneapolis, MN 55440

**Mr. George Marton**
Marketing Manager
Information Products Division
A.B. Dick Company
5700 Touhy Avenue
Chicago, IL 60648

**Ms. Barbara Mayes**
2100 Twickingham Drive
Muncie, IN 47304

**Mr. Martin Mendelsohn**
Executive Director
Land of Lincoln Legal Assistance
   Foundation, Inc.
516 East Monroe, 6-B Front
Springfield, IL 62701

**Mr. John D. Mitros**
Assistant Vice-President
Corporate Relations
Illinois Central Gulf Railroad
233 North Michigan Avenue
Chicago, IL 60601

**Mr. Beverly C. Moore Jr.**
1832 M Street, N.W. #101
Washington, D.C. 20036

**Mr. James M. Nicholson**
Nicholson and Carter
21 DuPont Circle, N.W.
Washington, D.C. 20036

**Mr. Frank Niehaus**
Assistant Director
Center for Consumer Education
Eastern Michigan University
Ypsilanti, MI 48197

**Ms. Cindy North**
Economist
Ball Corporation
Muncie, IN 47302

**Mr. Russell Ogden**
Department of Business Education
Eastern Michigan University
Ypsilanti, MI 48197

**Mr. Michael Pertschuk**
Senate Commerce Committee
Room 124
Russell (OSOB) Building
Washington, D.C. 20510

**Mr. William D. Plechaty**
Senior Vice-President
Personal Banking Department of
   Chicago Continental Illinois
   National Bank & Trust Company
231 South LaSalle Street
Chicago, IL 60690

**Mr. Cal Pond**
Vice-President
Safeway Stores, Inc.
4th & Jackson Streets
Oakland, CA 94660

**Mr. Daniel Powderly**
Consumer Representative
Celanese Fibers Company
1211 Avenue of the Americas
New York, NY 10036

**Ms. Jane Ranshaw**
NACBS
220 South State Street, Room 1318
Chicago, IL   60604

**Ms. Lee Rettig**
Liggett and Myers
4100 Roxero Road
Durham, NC   27704

**Mr. John C. Roberts**
Zenith Radio Corporation
1900 North Austin Avenue
Chicago, IL   60639

**Mr. Ivan Ross**
2061 Utah Avenue, South
Minneapolis, MN   55426

**Mr. G.R. Satzgaber**
Consumer Affairs Manager
General Foods
250 North Street
White Plains, NY   10625

**Professor S.P. Sethi**
School of Business Administration
305 Barrows Hall
University of California at Berkeley
Berkeley, CA   94720

**Ms. Esther Shapiro**
Director
Consumer Affairs Department
809 City County Building
Detroit, MI   48226

**Mr. R.W. Siebrasse**
Vice-President & Director of Marketing
CPC International, Inc.
International Plaza
Englewood Cliffs, NJ   07632

**Mr. Mark Silbergeld**
Consumers Union
1714 Massachusetts Avenue, N.W.
Washington, D.C.   20036

**Mr. Russell W. Smith**
Customer Relations Manager
Standard Oil of Indiana
200 East Randolph Street
Chicago, IL   60601

**Mr. Bud Spalding**
Sangamon State University
Springfield, IL   62700

**Mr. James E. Stafford**
Chairman
Department of Marketing – 339M
College of Business Administration
University of Houston
Cullen Boulevard
Houston, TX   77004

**Ms. Linda Standridge**
Consumer and Marketing Division
J.C. Penney Company
New York, NY   10000

**Professor Louis W. Stern**
Graduate School of Management
Nathaniel Leverone Hall
Northwestern University
Evanston, IL   60201

**Mr. R.A. Stevenson**
Director of Government & Public
   Relations
S.S. Kresge
3100 West Big Beaver Road
Troy, MI   48084

**Professor Hans B. Thorelli**
School of Business
Indiana University
Bloomington, IN   47401

**Mr. Gerald P. Thurmond**
Administrative Vice-President &
    Secretary
Gulf Oil Company
P.O. Box 2100
Houston, TX   77001

**Ms. Marian Tripp**
Director of Consumer Affairs
J. Walter Thompson
875 North Michigan Avenue
Chicago, IL   60611

**Mr. Tracy Weston, Esq.**
Public Communications
10203 Santa Monica Boulevard
Los Angeles, CA   90067

**Ms. Mary Lou Williamson**
Director of Consumer Service
Ball Corporation
Muncie, IN   47302

# Index

# Index

Abusive selling practices, 93
Action for Children's Television (ACT), 13
Administrative learning, 156-157, 163
Adversary process, 11, 15
Advertising, 77, 90, 99, 144-146
Advocacy, 9-11, 13, 86, 106-107
American Civil Liberties Union, 40
Antitrust, 116-118, 141
"Aroused citizenry" model, 133-134

Blind, agencies for, 2-3, 5

Class action, 92
"Community of interests" model, 130-131
Competition, 36, 45, 117, 118, 121, 142, 143
Consumer, information, 9, 58, 69-74, 90, 118, 142, 170; information problems, 168; movement, 1, 9, 42, 43-44, 49, 52 82, 89-98, 129-140, 150, 169; redress mechanisms, 168; satisfaction, 45, 52; sovereignty, 99, 105-109, 138, 139, 142, 170
Consumer Product Safety Commission (CPSC), 21-30, 84, 90, 108, 159
Consumer Protection Agency (CPA), 59, 61, 63-66, 68, 83, 133
Consumers Union, 1, 2, 41, 89
Corporate, power, 136; responsiveness, 158

Dynamic conservatism, 3

Ecology of organizations, 11

Federal Communications Commission (FCC), 35, 37-41, 85, 86, 132
Federal Trade Commission (FTC), 85, 91, 93, 95, 115-118, 132, 141, 145
Fraud, 91-93, 147

Government, state, 31-34, 51

Holder-in-due-course, 93
Homeostasis, 3

Idea in good currency, 4-5, 9
Inflation, 96, 97-98, 103, 115-116, 129
Information, 9, 58, 69-74, 90, 118, 142, 170
"Institutional" model, 132-133

Labor movement, 1
Learning, administrative, 156-157, 163; organization, 5-7; public, 7-8, 9; technical, 156-157

Major Appliance Consumer Action Panel (MACAP), 53-54
Mandatory origination rule, 38, 39, 40
Marketplace transaction problems, 168

Organization learning, 5-7

Political control, 43
Product, diversity problems, 168; externality issues, 168; safety, 21-30, 50, 84, 90, 108, 159
Public learning, 7-8, 9

Rational center-periphery model, 7-8

Safety, economic impact, 28; ethic, 24-25; product, 21-25, 28-29, 50, 90, 108
Selective inattention, 3
Small claims courts, 95
Social, audit, 120, 153; change, 59; movement, 158
Socialism, 142, 149
Socioeconomic Operating Statement (SEOS), 120-121, 125
Socioeconomic performance audit, 123-124

Technical learning, 156-157

Warranties, 45-55

# About the Contributors

**Donald A. Schon** was educated at the Sorbonne in Paris (1949-50), Yale University (B.A. 1951), Harvard (M.A. 1952), and Harvard University (Ph.D. in Philosophy, 1955). He is a Ford Professor of Urban Studies and Education at the Massachusetts Institute of Technology. Dr. Schon has had broad experience in a number of positions. He has served as president of the Organization for Social and Technical Innovation—OST (1966-1973); director of the Institute for Applied Technology, National Bureau of Standards (1964-1966); and a staff member of Arthur D. Little, Inc. (1957-1963). He is a member of the Commission on the Year 2000 and the American Academy of Arts and Sciences. Dr. Schon is the author of *Education for Effective Action* (with Chris Argyris, 1973) and *Beyond the Stable State* (1971).

**R. David Pittle** received the B.S. degree from the University of Maryland, and the M.S. and Ph.D. degrees in electrical engineering from the University of Wisconsin. He was an assistant professor of electrical engineering at Carnegie-Mellon University from 1969-1973. Dr. Pittle is serving a five-year term as a member of the Consumer Product Safety Commission. Before coming to the commission, Dr. Pittle had gained valuable experience in the field of consumerism by heading a 1,500 member citizens' committee in Pittsburgh entitled the Alliance for Consumer Protection.

**Celia A. Maloney** received the B.A. from Colorado State University in political science. She served as assistant to the Colorado Senate majority leadership from 1961 to 1962, and has worked in marketing and sales. In 1973 she was appointed consumer advocate in the Office of the Governor, state of Illinois. Ms. Maloney's volunteer activities include work with the Independent Voters of Illinois; the Children's Memorial Hospital in Chicago; and service as a fund raiser for the Crusade of Mercy and the Chicago Maternity Center. She is a board member of the Committee on Illinois Government, and a member of the 43rd Ward Citizens' Committee in Chicago.

**Steven R. Rivkin** was educated at Harvard University and Harvard Law School. He received the LL.B. in 1962. In his study and practice of law, Mr. Rivkin has concentrated in the areas of administrative, constitutional, and anti-trust law, and radio and television regulations. He is an expert in the area of cable television and is actively involved in the organization of cable television systems as well as the regulations involved in their establishment and use.

During his professional career, Mr. Rivkin has served on the White House staff in the Executive Office of Science and Technology during both the Kennedy and Johnson administrations. His published works include many articles and the books *Technology Unbound: Transfering Scientific and Engi-neering Resources from Defense to Civilian Purposes; Building Code Burden;* and *Cable TV: A Guide to Federal Regulations.*

**John C. Secrest** received the B.A. from Ohio Wesleyan University and the M.B.A. from the Harvard Business School. He is Group Vice-President, Staff and Inter-national Division, of American Motors Corporation and he has also served in the following capacities with American Motors Corporation; vice-president, corpor-ate staff; vice-president, finance; vice-president and general manager, appliance division; and vice-president, purchasing. Previous professional experience includes thirteen years with the Ford Motor Company, Ford Division in Finance and Purchasing. Mr. Secrest is also a member and past president of the Ohio Wesleyan University Alumni Club (Detroit area), director of the Harvard Business School Club of Detroit, vice-chairman of the United Negro College Fund (Michigan campaign), and a member of the Board of Directors for Southeast Michigan Junior Achievement.

**Daniel J. Krumm** is President and Treasurer of the Maytag Company and a member of the firm's Board of Directors. He is also president of the Maytag Company, Ltd., Toronto, a Canadian subsidiary. Mr. Krumm is a trustee of the Maytag Company Foundation, Inc., a member of Grand View College (Des Moines) Board of Directors; a member of the Maytag Management Club; a former board member of the Newton Chamber of Commerce; and a past president of the Iowa Chapter of the American Marketing Association.

**Peter T. Jones** received the LL.B. degree from Harvard University in 1957. He has served with the Kennedy and Johnson administrations in Washington, first as executive assistant to AID Director Harry Labouisse, later as deputy assistant secretary of commerce for trade, policy, and financial policy, and finally as deputy to Secretary of Commerce Luther Hodges. Mr. Jones joined Marcor and Montgomery Ward as Vice-President of Legal and Government Affairs in 1971. In addition to his professional duties, he is a member of the Council on Foreign Relations in New York, and is also active as a member of the Board of Directors of the American Retail Federation, the National Retail Merchants Association and the Council on Foreign Relations in Chicago.

Publications include numerous articles on U.S. trade policy over the years, a recent piece on multinational corporations and Latin America, published in *Business International*, and the research and initial draft of articles and a book on foreign policy entitled *Ideas,People, & Peace* (Harpers) for Chester Bowles.

**William Haddon, Jr.**, is President of the Insurance Institute for Highway Safety, Washington, D.C. He was director of the now National Highway Traffic Safety Administration, a position he held from his appointment by President Johnson in 1966 until 1969. Dr. Haddon built the extensive range of programs called for by the Congress in the two safety acts of 1966. This included the development

of the national standards for state and community highway safety programs, as
well as the initial standards for motor vehicles and their equipment. A physician
with degrees from the Massachusetts Institute of Technology, Harvard Medical
School, and the Harvard School of Public Health, Dr. Haddon is an authority on
the ecology of environmental hazards and on measures to reduce the damage
to people and property associated with them. Prior to his service with the federal
government, he was with the New York State Department of Health for ten
years. His scientific publications, predominantly dealing with public health,
have been extensive. Haddon has received numerous awards, including the
American Public Health Association's 1969 Bronfman Prize for Public Health
Achievement and the 1969 MODERN MEDICINE Distinguished Achievement
Award, ". . . in recognition of outstanding contributions to the progress of medicine as exemplified by his trailblazing scientific research in causes of traffic
trauma and administrative efforts to promote highway safety."

**Stephen A. Greyser** is a graduate of Harvard University (B.A.) and the Harvard
Business School (M.B.A. and D.B.A.). He teaches advertising and consumer
behavior at Harvard Business School and is executive director of the Marketing
Science Institute, a non-profit research center in the field of marketing associated with the Harvard Business School. He is also editorial board secretary of
the *Harvard Business Review*, on which he has served as assistant editor and
research director.

Professor Greyser is responsible for six books on marketing and advertising,
including *Advertising in America: The Consumer View* (co-authored) and *Cases
in Advertising and Communications Management*. He is a frequent interpreter
of consumerism's impacts on marketing, for both the business and public policy
communities. He has written extensively on consumerism and has prepared the
recently published *Harvard Business Review* reprint series *Understanding and
Meeting Consumerism's Challenges*. Active in professional associations, Professor Greyser is a past national director of the American Marketing Association,
past president of the American Academy of Advertising, and is on the Advisory
Council of the Association for Consumer Research.

**Mark Green** is the director of Ralph Nader's Corporate Accountability Research
Group. He is a graduate of Cornell (1967) and Harvard Law School (1970),
where he was editor-in-chief of the *Harvard Civil Rights Liberties Law Review*.
He has written or edited the following: *The Closed Enterprise System, Who
Runs Congress?; With Justice for Some; Corporate Power in America; The
Monopoly Makers; Verdicts on Lawyers;* and *The Other Government: The Un-
seen Power of Washington Lawyers*. Articles by him have appeared in the *Yale
Law Journal, New Review of Books, New York Times Book Review, New
Republic, Nation, Progressive, Village Voice,* and *New York* magazine.

**Philip G. Schrag** received the B.A. degree from Harvard University and the
LL.B. from the Yale Law School. He is professor of law at Columbia University

and teaches a clinical seminar in "Public Interest Advocacy" and a course in "Consumer Protection."

Prior to joining the faculty at Columbia, Dr. Schrag was the assistant counsel for the NAACP Legal Defense and Educational Fund, Inc. He has also served as a consumer advocate for the city of New York. He is the author of articles on such topics as Truth in Lending, Class Actions, Bankruptcy Law, and the Rights of Consumers. His books include *Public Interest and Advocacy: Materials for Clinical Legal Education* (with Meltsner), and *Counsel for the Deceived*.

**James S. Turner** received the LL.D. degree from Ohio State University in 1969 and then worked as a staff member for Ralph Nader on consumerism activities until 1971. Mr. Turner has had an active record of involvement in the consumerism movement. He has been a consultant to the National Heart and Lung Institute and is a consumer liaison to the Federal Trade Commission and the founder and codirector of Consumer Action for Improved Food and Drugs.

Mr. Turner has authored the book *Chemical Feast*, which is a report on the Food and Drug Administration, and is preparing another book that deals with the role and place of the consumerism movement in the American economic system.

**Herbert S. Landsman** is executive vice-president and a member of the Board of Directors of Federated Department Stores, Inc. He was educated at the University of Paris (1939), Dartmouth (B.A., 1940), and Harvard University (M.A., 1941).

Mr. Landsman is extremely active in business associations and civic activities and was previously a member of the American Management Association. He is director of the National Retail Merchants Association and a member of the Presidential Commission on Reorganization of the Post Office.

**Lewis A. Engman** received the LL.B. degree from the Harvard Law School in 1961. He is the chairman of the Federal Trade Commission and is the youngest person ever to head that agency. Before going to Washington, Chairman Engman was associated with a Grand Rapids law firm. In 1970, he became the legislator counsel for the President's Special Assistant for Consumer Affairs and later that same year was appointed General Counsel. In 1971 he was appointed Assistant Director of the White House Domestic Council.

**David F. Linowes** has been an adjunct professor of management at New York University and, during the 1973-74 academic year, he was the Distinguished Arthur Young Visiting Professor at the University of Illinois at Urbana–Champagne. Positions that Mr. Linowes has held in the accounting and management consultation fields have included chairman of the Trial Board of The American Institute of Certified Public Accountants; consultant and secretary to John W. Gardner, Department of Health, Education and Welfare, and consultant to the U.S. State Department and the United Nations. His publications include *Managing Growth Through Acquisition* (1968) and *Strategies for Survival* (1973).

**Richard C. Edwards** received the Ph.D. in economics from Harvard University in 1972. He is a research associate at the Harvard Graduate School of Education and assistant professor of economics at the University of Massachusetts.

Dr. Edwards has published extensively, including articles in the *American Economic Review* and the *Journal of Economic History*, as well as other professional journals. He is coauthor (with Michael Reich and Thomas Weisskopt) of *The Capitalist System*. He is the editor (with David Gordon and Michael Reich) of a volume of essays entitled *Labor Market Segmentation* and is working on a new book, tentatively entitled *Monopoly Capitalism and the Problems of Control in the Firm*.

**Richard D. Murphy** received the B.A. degree from Grinnel College in 1966 and the Ph.D. in economics from the University of Michigan in 1972. While at the University of Michigan, he was the Woodrow Wilson Fellow during 1966-67. While on leave from a position as assistant professor of economics at the University of Michigan, Dr. Murphy is serving as the special assistant to F.M. Scherer, director or economics, Federal Trade Commission. In this position, Dr. Murphy is in charge of economic analysis of consumer protection programs and cases.

**Raymond A. Bauer** received the B.A. degree from Northwestern University, and the M.A. and Ph.D. degrees from Harvard University. Since 1957 he has been a professor of business administration at the Harvard Business School. His professional experience includes work as a senior consultant on the National Goals Research Staff, the White House (1970), and consultant to Arthur D. Little, Inc. He is active in a variety of organizations in which he has held numerous offices over the years. They include the American Association of Advertising Agencies, the American Psychological Association, the National Academy of Sciences, the American Academy of Arts and Sciences, the Council on Economic Priorities, and the General Accounting Office. He is the author of numerous articles and books.

**David B. Kiser** is a consultant with Cambridge Research Institute in Cambridge, Massachusetts. He received the B.A. in management and political science from the Massachusetts Institute of Technology and the D.B.A. from Harvard Graduate School of Business Administration. Dr. Kiser's other writings include contributions to the *Chief Executive's Handbook* and general observations about the role and conduct of large corporations in modern society. His interests center around organizational responses to changes in public policy, and the role of social and political considerations in antitrust litigation and remedies.

# About the Editors

**Mary Gardiner Jones** is vice president–Consumer Affairs of Western Union Telegraphy Company. She received the J.D. degree from Yale University Law School and has been a practicing attorney with New York Law firms and the Antitrust Division of the Department of Justice. Ms. Jones served for nine years on the Federal Trade Commission (1964–1973) and from 1974–1975 was a professor in both the College of Law and in the College of Commerce and Business Administration at the University of Illinois. She has contributed articles to various legal, business, and financial periodicals, including the *George Washington Law Review, Law and Computer Technology,* and *Journal of Consumer Affairs.*

**David M. Gardner** received the B.S.C. degree from the University of Iowa and the M.S. and Ph.D. degrees in business administration from the University of Minnesota. Prior to his graduate education, he was employed by the J.C. Penny Company. He is a professor of business administration and marketing at the University of Illinois, Urbana-Champaign. Professor Gardner has served as a behavioral science advisor to the Federal Trade Commission and was president of the Association for Consumer Research in 1976.